EDITED BY
CHRISTOPHER BAKER,
BETH R. CRISP AND ADAM DINHAM

# RE-IMAGINING RELIGION AND BELIEF

21st-century policy and practice

POLICY PRESS SHORTS RESEARCH

First published in Great Britain in 2018 by

Policy Press
University of Bristol
1-9 Old Park Hill
Bristol
BS2 8BB
UK
t: +44 (0)117 954 5940
pp-info@bristol.ac.uk
www.policypress.co.uk

North America office:
Policy Press
c/o The University of Chicago Press
1427 East 60th Street
Chicago, IL 60637, USA
t: +1 773 702 7700
f: +1 773 702 9756
sales@press.uchicago.edu
www.press.uchicago.edu

© Policy Press 2018

British Library Cataloguing in Publication Data
A catalogue record for this book is available from the British Library.

Library of Congress Cataloging-in-Publication Data
A catalog record for this book has been requested.

ISBN 978-1-4473-4709-5   (hardback)
ISBN 978-1-4473-4711-8   (ePub)
ISBN 978-1-4473-4712-5   (Mobi)
ISBN 978-1-4473-4710-1   (ePDF)

The right of Christopher Baker, Beth R. Crisp and Adam Dinham to be identified as editors of this work has been asserted by them in accordance with the Copyright, Designs and Patents Act 1988.

All rights reserved: no part of this publication may be reproduced, stored in a retrieval system, or transmitted in any form or by any means, electronic, mechanical, photocopying, recording, or otherwise without the prior permission of Policy Press.

The statements and opinions contained within this publication are solely those of the authors and not of the University of Bristol or Policy Press. The University of Bristol and Policy Press disclaim responsibility for any injury to persons or property resulting from any material published in this publication.

Policy Press works to counter discrimination on grounds of gender, race, disability, age and sexuality.

Cover design by Policy Press
Front cover: image kindly supplied by www.alamy.com
Printed and bound in Great Britain by CPI Group (UK) Ltd, Croydon, CR0 4YY
Policy Press uses environmentally responsible print partners

# Contents

| | | |
|---|---|---|
| List of contributors | | iv |
| **PART 1: RE-IMAGINING RELIGION AND BELIEF SPACES** | | |
| one | The need to re-imagine religion and belief<br>*Adam Dinham, Christopher Baker and Beth R. Crisp* | 3 |
| two | Re-negotiating religion and belief in the public square:<br>Definitions, debates, controversies<br>*Christopher Baker and Adam Dinham* | 15 |
| three | Geographical landscapes of religion<br>*Paul Cloke and Andrew Williams* | 33 |
| four | 'Spatial methodology' in religion and belief research:<br>The example of a study of Twelver Shii Muslim networks in Britain<br>*Oliver Scharbrodt* | 55 |
| **PART 2: RE-IMAGINING PUBLIC POLICY AND PRACTICE** | | |
| five | Law and religion: A survey of cases in the UK and what they reveal<br>*Lucy Vickers* | 77 |
| six | Reading religion through the lessons of legal decisions and<br>reactions to them<br>*Lori G. Beaman* | 95 |
| seven | Religious dimensions of postcolonial policy in Australia<br>*Mark G. Brett* | 115 |
| eight | Re-imagining the place of religion in the workplace:<br>The example of Australian social work<br>*Beth R. Crisp* | 131 |
| nine | Religious literacy in welfare and civil society: A Nordic perspective<br>*Annette Leis-Peters* | 145 |
| **PART 3: RE-IMAGINING THE FUTURE** | | |
| ten | Policy futures for religion and belief<br>*Christopher Baker, Beth R. Crisp and Adam Dinham* | 171 |
| Afterword | *Grace Davie* | 183 |
| Index | | 193 |

# List of contributors

**Christopher Baker** is William Temple Professor of Religion and Public Life at Goldsmiths, University of London, and Director of Research at the William Temple Foundation, UK.

**Lori G. Beaman** holds the Canada Research Chair in Religious Diversity and Social Change in the Department of Classics and Religious Studies at the University of Ottawa, Canada.

**Mark G. Brett** is Professor of Hebrew Bible at Whitley College and the University of Divinity, Melbourne, Australia.

**Paul Cloke** is Professor of Human Geography in the Department of Geography at the University of Exeter, UK.

**Beth R. Crisp** is Professor and Discipline Leader for Social Work in the School of Health and Social Development, Deakin University, Australia.

**Grace Davie** is an Emeritus Professor in the Sociology of Religion at the University of Exeter, UK.

**Adam Dinham** is Professor of Faith and Public Policy and Director of the Faiths and Civil Society Unit, Goldsmiths, University of London, UK.

## LIST OF CONTRIBUTORS

**Annette Leis-Peters** is Vice-Dean of the Faculty of Theology, Diaconia and Leadership Studies and Associate Professor of Sociology of Religion at VID Specialized University, Oslo, Norway.

**Oliver Scharbrodt** is Professor of Islamic Studies in the Department of Theology and Religion at the University of Birmingham, UK.

**Lucy Vickers** is Professor of Law at Oxford Brookes University, UK, and Assistant Director of the Centre for Diversity Policy Research and Practice.

**Andrew Williams** is Lecturer in Human Geography in the School of Geography and Planning at Cardiff University, UK.

For Zachariah, with the deepest of thanks always,
to Anna Lockwood, Donna Bryant and their families

# PART 1:
# RE-IMAGINING RELIGION AND BELIEF SPACES

# ONE

# The need to re-imagine religion and belief

Adam Dinham, Christopher Baker and Beth R. Crisp

## Why do we need to re-imagine religion and belief?

Why re-imagine religion and belief? What's wrong with how we think about them now? This is the question at the root of this volume, made pressing by a greater visibility of religion and belief across the public sphere than for a generation, and a public policy freneticism about it that has been largely preoccupied with sex, money and violence (Dinham and Francis, 2015). Policies abound about inequality, cohesion, extremism, migration, abuse and unethical investments. These are reflected and sometimes magnified in media representations of dangerous Muslims on the one hand and marginalised Christians on the other (Lovheim, 2013). A lack of religious literacy has been one way of looking at this – observing a public sphere that struggles to cope with a growing diversity as well as visibility of religion and belief in every sector and setting (Dinham, 2017). How has this come about?

A combination of old binaries and powerful paradigms is critical to the explanation. They reside in academic disciplines and are reflected in policy norms that may have run out of road. The conundrum is that they no longer equip us for the challenges that are faced — of super-diversity, extremism and the continuing role of faith groups in the provision of increasingly critical social services.

The dominance of the secular paradigm is foremost, and is arguably Sociology's greatest success. It is at the root of Western difficulty with talking about religion. There appears to be a widespread and deep-rooted assumption at large that religion and belief are essentially in decline and likely to disappear. Nuanced and contested though the notion really is, this 'vanishing point' perspective of secularity informs much of what schools and universities teach, and how professions and leaderships practice, as the chapters that follow unpick. Yet as critics have noted, simple decline is too simple a tale. People are 'believing without belonging' (Davie, 1994), as well as the inverse of 'belonging without believing' (Hervieu-Léger, 2000). At the same time, a de-formalisation is observed that detaches people from institutions and reveals religion and belief as subject to the same consumerist and marketised behaviours and choices as exercised in other walks of life (Woodhead, 2012). Most (84%) of the global population reports a religion or belief (Pew Research Center, 2012). Europe's apparent secular decline is the exception not the rule (Davie, 2015). It turns out that the world is neither simply secular nor simply religious, but complexly both. As Weller (2009) points out in relation to Britain, it is more secular, more religious and more diverse at once. So secular assumptions — whether procedural or programmatic (Williams, 2006) — look increasingly like a dead end. Globalisation and migration put everyone in to a daily encounter with a diversity of religion, belief and non-belief, whether they like it or not, in every public sphere. An insistence on private, not public, religion looks shaky in that light. More religious diversity does not seem well met by more secularity.

Yet this is the other great binary that persists. Habermas' (2006) earlier proposal of the privacy of religion and his requirement that it appear in the public sphere only in the language of 'public reasons' is problematic in societies that find themselves needing to name religions and beliefs, engage with them, and increasingly to hold them to account. How can we both talk and not talk about religion and belief? The neutrality implied by 'public reasons' is itself in question anyway, since the non-religiousness of shared space is full instead of other normativities, beliefs and worldviews revolving around liberal and neoliberal commitments. Habermas himself developed the concept of the postsecular in the early years of this millennium in order to scope and interrogate this dynamically shifting religious and cultural modernity. As we unpack in greater detail in Chapter 2, for him, the postsecular represents a new 'self-understanding of society as a whole in which the vigorous continuation of religion in a continually secularizing environment must be reckoned with' (Habermas, 2005, p 26). For Habermas, the postsecular acknowledges several things – one, the resurgence of global religion due to immigration and growth in fundamentalist religion, especially Islam and Pentecostal Christianity; second, the decline in confidence in secular Enlightenment narratives of the modern liberal democratic state, the ideals and values of which have been hollowed out by neoliberal capitalism; third, issues of equality and human rights in respect of the approach to religious identities and beliefs in the public sphere; and fourth, the requirement for a new re-imagining of the relationship between the religious and the secular for the sake of a flourishing civil society and participative democracy. These four elements are highly relevant to the issues that this volume seeks to address.

## What's different about the 21st century?

Another major shift feeding into the genesis of this research network and this volume is the general recognition that the 21st century has generated a new form of modernity that is profoundly different to that devised and envisaged in the 19th and 20th centuries. There are several elements to this shift. The first is the exponential acceleration of the processes of globalised capitalism that combines both neoliberal deregulation with innovations in communication technology and travel to allow the maximum fluidity and frictionless crossing over geographic and cultural domains for the sake of market efficiency. This has created more intense flows of migration, ideology, innovation, investment and knowledge that show little respect for existing forms of local identity or community.

The increasingly interconnected nature of this new hyper-globalised modernity (what Beck, 2010, calls 'Modernity 2') has also generated hitherto unparalleled levels of risk, as good or intentional policy decisions often get diverted by the complexity and unaccountability of new networks of decision-making and agency. The financial crash of 2008 was a global event that epitomised this new modernity, and its impacts continue to reverberate ominously a decade later. These negative impacts include growing social and economic inequality, and a heightened sense of anxiety and fragmentation at the apparent loss of any political party or strategy that will restore a sense of control and order. This largely explains the dip in trust in more liberal and democratic forms of political engagement that has led to the rise in support for parties or movements offering simple and comforting solutions to complex globalised problems (epitomised by Brexit and the rise of despotic leaders like Donald Trump in the US and Recep Tayyip Erdoğan in Turkey). Religion and belief are once again brought to the fore, as a source of personal consolation in times of fear and anxiety, as an ideological prop to a 'pure nation/culture' narrative, or as a diffuse but powerful presence in new alternative movements of participation and democracy.

Meanwhile, Western understandings of secular modernity following the European Enlightenment (what Beck, 2010, calls 'Modernity 1') lose global traction in favour of geo-political shifts eastwards towards growing populations, economies and cultures that don't subscribe to rigid norms of separation between religion and belief and the public and the private. The blurring of hitherto rigidly imagined intellectual boundaries in 'Modernity 1' has also given way to real-world blurring associated with 'Modernity 2'. How complex, diverse, increasingly crowded and also privatised public spaces are being contested and shared in the real world presents constant challenges to both established policy and academic ideas, which struggle to keep touch with these new realities. This real-world experience highlights the usefulness of the concept of the intersectionality (Crenshaw, 1989) of identities that overlap within and between people and that are fluid and shifting. This helps us understand religion and belief, not as blocks of unchanging tradition, but as lived experience in ordinary everyday lives that spills over and directly influences other aspects of private and public modernity.

## Why the growth in religion and belief talk, and why across academic disciplines?

It is perhaps unsurprising that greater visibility of religion and belief in the public sphere is reflected in a similar growth in engagement in a broad range of academic disciplines. Universities are frequently expected to provide intellectual leadership on matters of public interest and concern to the communities in which they are located. At the same time, student and employer expectations that graduates are 'work ready' increasingly includes the capacity to effectively work with individuals and communities with diverse religious beliefs and practices.

The re-emergence of religion and belief is a new twist on medieval notions in which the study of Theology was considered integral to the idea of a university. The rapid expansion of higher education in many countries in the 20th century led to the contention that a 'real' university was one that taught Medicine and Law. At the same time, Social Science disciplines, such as Psychology and Sociology, have claimed the expertise as to the essence of human existence, once held by Theology. In a neoliberal era, the continuing existence of faculties of Theology and Religious Studies is often dependent on financial considerations — that is, whether the disciplines bring in sufficient funds to the institution.

Academic study of matters religious has never entirely occurred in faculties of Theology and Religious Studies. But just as Theology and Religious Studies have been marginalised in many universities, scholarship about religion in other disciplines has frequently been dismissed or disregarded as having little relevance in supposedly secular societies, even when the majority of the population, at least in private, identifies with religious institutions, teachings and/or cultures.

All three of us work in avowedly secular universities that have no Theology and Religious Studies faculty, but in 2017 they introduced new units of academic study in religion, something that would have been unimaginable just a few years ago.

Our own experiences and observations of a changing culture in the academy towards matters associated with religion and belief in the broader society has been the impetus for the work that this volume presents. Academic expertise once considered marginal and of little consequence to society is increasingly recognised as making an essential contribution. Another change we have observed is that scholars of religion and belief, once almost exclusively people for whom their own religion was of personal importance, is increasingly attracting scholars of no, or no stated, religion.

Despite our own experiences of living and working in a number of countries, of working in different disciplinary settings, as well as our differences in a range of socio-demographic characteristics, each of us has struggled with the overly simplified paradigms about faith and religion in which we were socialised, both personally and academically. As such, we and the other contributors to this volume reflect the boundary dissolving and crossing that we have come to recognise as essential if we are to take seriously questions of religion and faith in the societies in which we live.

## Why does it matter for policy?

A critical question for religion and belief in the public sphere is whether old forms of thinking result in old forms of policy that misalign the real religion and belief landscape and policy about them. Thinking as a secular polis in which religion is traditional, private and declining is likely to determine policy that misconceives the opportunities and risks. It accounts for a focus on religion and belief as oppressive, sexist, homophobic and violent, as reflected in attempted policy solutions in equality law and initiatives for the prevention of violent extremism. Each implicitly emphasises the risk side of the equation. Religion and belief diversity is engaged as a problem to be solved – by banning burkas (in France), restricting the travel of Muslims (in the US), and allowing employers to forbid the wearing of religious symbols (in the EU).

In other cases, the opposite happens and faith groups are cast as heroic providers of community and social services that states cannot afford or deliver without them (Putnam, 2000; Dinham et al, 2006). In the US this has frequently resulted in heated debate about the propriety of faith-based services that may be exclusive to people of the providing faith, or come with evangelical strings attached. Yet rose-tinted views of churches full of volunteers are also cut across by evidence of declining congregations of old ladies who are dying and not being replaced (Day, 2017). Where, then, is the army of volunteers that is imagined? Is it where policy-makers think it is, and what happens when resources are targeted there and very little happens?

It has been observed that we are on religion where we were on race in the 1960s, gender in the 1970s and sexual orientation in the 1980s, 1990s and 2000s (Dinham, 2017). None of those identities is solved either, but there are at least bottom lines and ways of talking about them that make the conversations visible and possible. By contrast, there are few policy norms on religion and belief and ill-tempered debates are falling into the gaps. Law is one site of this struggle and reflects old forms of thinking. Equality law constructs religion and belief as risky identities to be protected. Freedom of religion provisions, such as those in the UN Universal Declaration of Human Rights, and in the US Constitution, go back much further and as such are also rooted in out-dated assumptions of private religion in otherwise secular states. This challenges the public sphere to come to terms with new ways of thinking that engage with a world that is religious and secular, private and public, after all.

## What are the implications for practice?

While a conventional approach to policy analysis is to analyse a set of reforms (actual or proposed) in respect of how they solve the stated problem, a more illuminating approach is to consider how a problem is construed in the first place. Hence, it has been proposed that 'rather than reacting to "problems", governments are active in the creation (or production) of policy "problems'" (Bacchi, 2009, p 1), which in turn suggest a set of solutions. Understanding these differing perspectives may give us some insights about the place of religion and belief in a society, and the forces that seek to constrain or promote their existence and proliferation. This, in turn, requires exposing the underlying assumptions or presuppositions associated with this form of problem representation and considering how the 'problem' has come to be represented in this way. This then leads to considering the effects that are produced from a particular representation of a 'problem', and includes asking questions such as:

- How is the problem understood?
- Who understands the problem in this way?
- Who benefits from this being the accepted understanding of the problem?
- Who is blamed for the problem occurring?
- Who is harmed by this understanding of the problem?
- How else can this problem be understood? (Bacchi, 2009)

Such analysis of the practice implications of policy not only uncover deliberate discrimination of people or communities due to their religion or beliefs but also indirect discrimination that may not have been intended, as can occur by the prescription or proscription of particular items of clothing or setting of working hours.

Although issues of religion and belief can emerge in all areas of policy and professional practice, practitioners in education, law and justice, and health and social care are particularly likely to have to deal with the ramifications of policies that have not appropriately understood the complexities and lived experiences of people of minority religions or beliefs. Globalisation and migration are the most obvious, but far from the only contributors to the religious hyper-diversity, which daily challenges many public professionals.

There is clearly a need for evidence-based policy that supports the needs of religiously diverse communities, and that has the capacity to not entrench existing stereotypes. However, this, in turn, may require new methodologies in forming policies, including relevant consultation processes, to ensure new policies and practices do not recreate religion and beliefs as inherently problematic.

## Structure of the book

In the remainder of Part 1: Re-imagining religion and belief spaces, we lay out the nature of the new debates and controversies around the public expression of religion and belief in both academia and policy unearthed by the data from the UK Arts and Humanities Research Council (AHRC) Re-imagining Religion and Belief project (Chapter 2 by Christopher Baker and Adam Dinham). This begins to locate some of these policy interactions with lived experiences of religion and belief within new interdisciplinary frameworks of theory and research within the Arts and Humanities. These include the turn towards practices and landscapes of religion and belief in critical geography (Chapter 3, Paul Cloke and Andrew Williams) and the spatial turn within Islamic religious studies (Chapter 4, Oliver Scharbrodt).

In Part 2: Re-imagining public policy and practice, we then explore the ways in which religion and belief is both framed and then unpacked for public consumption by legal frameworks in the West (Chapter 5, Lucy Vickers [UK] followed by Chapter 6, Lori G. Beaman [Canada] and Chapter 7, Mark G. Brett [Australia]). The case study of law highlights some of the ways in which the frameworks, procedures and discourses of secular modernity reify religion and belief in ways that no longer resonate with its deformalised expression. Brett, in particular, focuses on the theological turn towards post-colonialism and indigenous rights in Australia, and how this might enhance and develop policy in the area of land rights and access to public services. It is then followed by two chapters that engage with areas of policy that adopt a more grounded approach to the lived expression of religion and belief among ordinary members of the public and within faith communities – namely, social work in Australia and care and welfare services in Norway (see Chapter 8 by Beth R. Crisp and Chapter 9 by Annette Leis-Peters respectively).

Part 3: Re-imagining the future explores how a new openness to religion in the sphere of public policy can contribute to individuals, communities and whole societies being able to imagine and work towards positive new futures. The final chapter by the editors identifies a new set of policy futures for religion and belief in respect to how and where old ways of imagining and managing religion and belief in the public square are giving way to new ideas and experiences. These are not only generating new policy ideas, but also new forms of language and idiom with which to talk about these 'matters of concern' in our new modernity.

## References

Bacchi, C. (2009) *Analysing policy: What's the problem represented to be?*, Frenchs Forest, NSW: Pearson.

Beck, U. (2010) *A god of one's own*, Cambridge: Polity Press.

Crenshaw, K. (1989) 'Demarginalizing the intersection of race and sex: A Black feminist critique of antidiscrimination doctrine, feminist theory and antiracist politics', *University of Chicago Legal Forum*, vol 140, pp 139-67.

Davie, G. (1994) *Religion in Britain since 1945: Believing without belonging*, Oxford: Blackwell Publishing.

Davie, G. (2015) *Religion in Britain: A persistent paradox* (2nd edn), Chichester: Wiley Blackwell.

Day, A. (2017) *The religious lives of older laywomen: The last active Anglican generation*, Oxford: Oxford University Press.

Dinham, A. (2017) 'Developing religious literacy in higher education', in K. Aune and J. Stevenson (eds) *Religion and higher education in Europe and North America*, London: Routledge, pp 202-15.

Dinham, A. and Francis, M. (eds) (2015) *Religious literacy in policy and practice*, Bristol: Policy Press.

Dinham, A., Farnell, R., Finneron, D. and Furbey, R. (2006) *Faith as social capital: Connecting or dividing?*, Bristol: Policy Press.

Habermas, J. (2005) 'Equal treatment of cultures and the limits of postmodern liberalism', *Journal of Political Philosophy*, vol 13, no 1, pp 1-28.

Habermas, J. (2006) 'Religion in the public sphere', *European Journal of Philosophy*, vol 14, no 1, pp 1-25.

Hervieu-Léger, D. (2000) *Religion as a chain of memory*, New Brunswick, NJ: Rutgers University Press.

Lovheim, M. (ed) (2013) *Media, religion and gender: Key issues and challenges*, London: Routledge.

Pew Research Center (2012) *The global religious landscape: A report on the size and distribution of the world's major religious groups as of 2010*, Washington, DC: Pew Research Center (www.pewforum.org/files/2014/01/global-religion-full.pdf).

Putnam, R.D. (2000) *Bowling alone: The collapse and revival of American community*, New York: Simon & Schuster.

Weller, P. (2009) 'How participation changes things: "Inter-faith", "multi-faith" and a new public imaginary', in A. Dinham, R. Furbey and V. Lowndes (eds) *Faith in the public realm: Controversies, policies and practices*, Bristol: Policy Press, pp 63-81.

Williams, R. (2006) 'Secularism, faith and freedom', Presented at the Pontifical Academy of Social Sciences, Rome, 23 November (http://rowanwilliams.archbishopofcanterbury.org/articles.php/1175/rome-lecture-secularism-faith-and-freedom).

Woodhead, L. (2012) 'Introduction', in L. Woodhead and R. Catto, Rebecca (eds) *Religion and change in modern Britain*, London: Routledge, pp 1-33.

# TWO

# Re-negotiating religion and belief in the public square: Definitions, debates, controversies

Christopher Baker and Adam Dinham

## Introduction

In the previous chapter we laid out some of the intellectual, social and political imperatives for a more informed and nuanced policy discussion about the increase in the public role and impacts of religion and belief that has emerged with the arrival of the new millennium. We now turn to an analysis of the data gathered from the UK Arts and Humanities Research Council (AHRC)-funded interdisciplinary research project, Re-imagining Religion and Belief for Policy and Practice that ran from 2014 to 2016, which has framed the new interdisciplinary analysis in this volume.

## Methodology

The Re-imagining Religion and Belief for Policy and Practice research network aimed to critically map a wide range of contemporary conceptions of religion and belief, and to translate, disseminate and calibrate this mapping for policy audiences. We sought, as the principle researchers, to engage new thinking about religion and belief with policy-makers' ideas in those key policy fields related to religion and belief that are especially prominent: security and cohesion; community and neighbourhood; education; welfare and the third sector; international development; and health and social care. The network curated information sharing and debates on religion and belief from several current disciplines, including Religious Studies, Political Philosophy, Public, Practical and Political Theology, Cultural Studies, Anthropology and Sociology of Religion, Social and Public Policy, and Critical Urban Geography.

The process of mapping, reflecting and translation into policy terms had four iterations, designed to triangulate as much as possible our inductive mapping of key ideas and themes across the different disciplines. The first iteration involved 'landmark' semi-structured interviews with 18 leading critical thinkers in the study of religions and beliefs. These thinkers were selected not only for their global reputation, but also because many could be considered to be public intellectuals, transcending as well as epitomising key thinking in their disciplines. It was this quality of perspective we were seeking to engage. Each participant responded to three questions: How do you characterise the present debate/dialogue concerning religion and the public sphere in your field? What are the key pinch-points and new insights? Where is the study of religions and beliefs going to go in the next five to ten years?

Next, in May 2015, there was an intensive three-day residential colloquium where the findings from the landmark interviews were deepened and furthered by a multidisciplinary group of 15 academic experts. The group included five international participants (from Australia, Canada, Finland, Norway and the US) as well as seven doctoral or early-career researchers, already combining innovative cross-disciplinary work in their own studies of religions and beliefs, across Anthropology, Cultural Studies, Geography, Philosophy, Political

Science, Social and Public Policy, Religious Studies, Social Work, Sociology, and Theology.

The third phase focused on policy engagement. A group of eight participants, drawn from the fields of government/civil service, local authorities, faith-based social action and Councils of Voluntary Service, met for a one-day workshop at the House of Lords in the UK Parliament. Each participant was asked to give a 'lightning' presentation of 5-7 minutes outlining the ways in which religions and beliefs 'bite' in their setting. They then prioritised a shortlist of between five and ten practical changes to public policy in relation to religions and beliefs in these policy areas.

The final phase was an international road show to test out how the ideas emerging in a UK context might translate into public policy contexts elsewhere. One-day events were held in Ottawa, Canada (in May 2016), Oslo, Norway (in June 2016) and Melbourne, Australia (in November 2016). These combined the formats of the colloquia and the policy workshop to include a presentation of findings from the landmark interviews and discussion of their translatability, although this time transnationally.

## Findings

This section explores the preoccupations in contemporary thinking about religions and beliefs as they have emerged in our interviews and colloquia across 10 Arts, Humanities and Social Science disciplines. Four main areas emerge, each articulated through fields of public policy: welfare; participative governance; cohesion, integration and violence; and equality.

The complexity and variety of these spaces and discourses is framed within the concept of liminality. This is used to draw attention to the observation that this is a moment of change, a threshold, in which the relationship between disciplines may be ripe for renegotiation as they engage and re-engage internally and with each other with issues concerning religions and beliefs in new ways.

## *Anthropology*

The Charlie Hebdo attack in Paris, France, in January 2015 was a key catalyst for those reflecting on religions and beliefs from the perspective of current anthropological debates. This focused in particular on the issue of violence, but not in relation to extremism so much as violence to religious freedom in the 'liberal public square'. While extremist violence has attracted most media and policy attention and debate, the questions addressed by anthropologists are more concerned with the nature of the implicit and legitimised violence generated towards minority faiths by the hegemonic assumptions and practices of the liberal democratic nation-state. They identify stereotypical and negative assumptions as the constant and daily background noise against which more nuanced and complex views on religion and belief identities struggle to be heard and articulated. The thesis is posed that the West is in danger of losing its ability to conduct a liberal conversation (inclusive and respectful, but also challenging and critical) about the public role of religions and beliefs.

In response to this problematic, Anthropology reminds other disciplines that it comfortably works with a number of different perspectives and disciplines. Anthropology has, in the words of one interviewee, 'infused' its own disciplinary approach with those of other traditions, including theology, feminism, Marxism and structuralism:

> So really ... the most interesting anthropologists have been those who have been able to either take in or be receptive to ideas from other disciplines.... [Most] anthropologists are aware of this, and not too concerned about boundaries of their discipline.

Meanwhile, a traditional commitment to ethnographic fieldwork is seen as not only contextualising and breaking open often dense and abstract debates about the postsecular into its lived-out complexities and particularities; it also allows new sorts of questions to emerge that might help break the log-jam of debate in some areas of academia:

> The fact that anthropologists tend to do fieldwork has been important in the way in which it encouraged us to look at the detail in particular, and be open really to what will come so to speak. One doesn't go into the field with a priori questions, detailed questions. But a willingness to listen and to hear what the people or the place one is going to has to say to one. And in that way I think that one of the most interesting things that has developed in anthropology in religion has been ... the willingness to look out for new questions, and not be satisfied with a priori positions.

This draws attention to what is involved in opening up new spaces of interdisciplinarity about the role of religions and beliefs in a period of change and uncertainty. As the spectrum of lived expressions of religious and non-religious beliefs becomes more apparent through fieldwork, the question is raised as to whether the West can discover more effective forms of co-existence. One interviewee asks:

> Can religious traditions and the language that different people have inherited in different ways from those traditions ... contribute to enlightening us in ways that helps us both to resolve and to accommodate each other, but also to challenge each other? To think again rather than to get out of the way. I hope they will be more like that, and that means asking questions about the secular as well as the religious.

Other anthropological perspectives reported within this project challenge the implied preference for religion as a normative source of moral sentiments, citing evidence of the growth in 'no religion' identities in the West, especially among those under the age of 40 who appear to be rejecting institutional Christianity in large numbers. However, the anthropologists interviewed for the project concur with what other academic disciplines associate with the current period, namely, the loosening of identities with regard to either traditional or binary religious or secular traditions. Increasing numbers of people seem to be gravitating towards a religiously fuzzy, but politically and civically intentional, 'middle'.

## *Critical Geography*

Several respondents in our interviews highlighted an emerging interest in landscapes and geographies of religions and beliefs within Critical Geography. It was noted, however, that the debate still largely adopts a narrative that sees religious welfare, social care and justice movements as compensating for the gaps left behind by a retreating state rather than a phenomenon that is changing the public sphere in its own right. The 'spatial' turn within Sociology and Religious Studies based on close examination of the relationship between the material, the spatial and the imagined was noted by several interviewees. They reflected on the increasingly significant role played by religious individuals and communities in the creation of flourishing and resilient localities, especially in contexts of poverty and marginalisation. One contributor reflected that the decline of the political left in these communities has created new opportunities for religion to step into the vacuum:

> When I was growing up you could change the world through left politics. It's now short-changed. It's much harder to do it through the secular, political tradition. It's been defeated time and time again. And so religion stands out more because there's a kind of vacuum all around ... not just because it's there but also because it has a strong value base, and it offers people ... an anti-materialist analysis of the world in terms of having a good life, a community, solidarity. So it's some of the space the left used to fill.

Two further strands of interdisciplinary thinking emerge from a growing interest in these new geographies of religions and beliefs. The first is that religion's ability to flourish in an increasingly globalised and urbanised world challenges one of the basic assumptions of the 'secularisation thesis', namely, that processes of modernisation and technological innovation associated with urban planning and design render religious practices and discourses increasingly redundant and obsolete. Critical Geography recognises (along with other disciplines) that religion and modernity not only coexist, but are also symbolically intertwined, creating the material possibilities for new progressive alliances.

The second strand is that the fluidity and liminality of the public square means that 'the spatial' becomes the arena in which future configurations of the religious, spiritual and religious 'nones' are being contested, negotiated and translated in real time. Theoretical assumptions and conceptual frameworks located in more binary readings of the world are thus likely to be behind the curve of events that are now beyond the scope of a single disciplinary perspective to adequately ground. This makes the interdisciplinary reading of religions and beliefs in the public square all the more essential. One example is the emergence of new spaces of ethical and political convergence in which previously recognised ideological barriers appear to be dissolving. One contributor reflected that:

> There is some evidence that alternative imaginaries and practices are generating new ethical spaces and subjectivities. Geographies of postsecularity suggest that we are journeying into rather different subjectivities. What has captured the imagination of hard-nosed Marxists is the emergence of a new kind of ethics and "leave your differences at the door".

## *Political Philosophy*

In line with many other disciplinary perspectives, the preoccupation of Political Philosophy is the power of globalisation. As the boundaries of the nation-state become more blurred with the ascendency of the global network, there is a concomitant dismantling or blurring of boundaries at the disciplinary level. Claims to superior knowledge or epistemology are no longer valid. The global de-privatisation of religion puts pressure on traditional categories of political analysis and philosophy that emerged in the 19th and 20th centuries. A major question posed by political philosophers in this study concerns the implications of the 'hushed-up' voice of religion (Eder, 2006, p 1) coming back into the public square. The flux and intense changes that have emerged since the 2008 financial crash, and the political charge being increasingly attached to religion, was interpreted by one participant using the scientific norms of thermodynamic theory, which is also closely associated with new materialism:

> What I like about what's called the new materialism is that it's not a reductionistic, atomic materialism. For me it's about energy transformation.... Not just in political and economic terms but also in cosmological terms and thermodynamic terms. For me what I like about energy is that it can evade this dichotomy of matter and spirit so you can think about energy as flowing material, you can also think about it as spiritual as well.... For me to think about religion and politics and the public spheres and spaces that we engage and live in and enter into, I want to think about energy as what makes all of that possible. In a sense without reducing everything to a kind of reductionistic, deterministic view of energy, but a more complex one that works.

In this reading, the impacts of religions and beliefs in the public sphere are creatively interpreted using scientific norms and principles. They are seen as forces of energy interacting. This scientific analogy by which to interpret religion itself embodies a readiness for and opening up of new interdisciplinary thinking and analysis.

## *Theology*

The responses of the theologians in our cohort can be grouped into two categories. The first could be labelled as reflecting a 'pessimistic' response regarding the current role of religions and beliefs in the public sphere. The 'pessimist' position sees religions, but particularly Christianity, as being driven out of the public square by an aggressive secularism, often sponsored by the state and abetted by certain sections of media, opinion formers and academia. This viewpoint offers a trenchant critique that links secularism and neoliberalism with the creation of a public sphere in which citizens are imagined as social monads, for whom the stable solidarities fostered by institutions such as the family and the church are portrayed as infringements on individual freedoms and rights:

> We went through what you could call a humanist post-Christian phase where the values remain Christian, even though people were agnostic and some people were atheists. Now we've moved into a phase of far sharper contestation.... Look at the last bastion of Christian influence, the family. It remains central to our ideas of what a family should be. Now you could argue that secular forces, forces of the state and the market, are trying to break up family life, trying to appeal directly to individuals. Just as all intermediary institutions between the state and the individual have been eroded, now I think the family also is being undermined.

Others, who we might label 'realist', were more sanguine, seeing at least as many opportunities as challenges to harnessing a renewed interest in religion (and religious ideas) towards a new ethical consensus on the nature and purpose of the public square. One participant expressed the power relations between the religious and the secular in the memorable metaphor of the Jacuzzi versus the shower. The traditional Western model of modernity operates as a 'shower'. Religion is like a flow of water that can be specifically controlled and directed to certain areas, and those who do not want to be touched by it can chose to bypass or ignore that flow of water. However, under the new conditions of globalised modernity, religion is likened more to a Jacuzzi:

> It [religion] was a process through which we would be washed clean of our archaic and atavistic religious views. But I think in reality the context is more like a Jacuzzi in that everything is bubbling up from everywhere.

In other words, and in common with the disintegrating of boundaries' motif identified in other disciplines, the religious and the secular are increasingly less differentiated, and instead, are more co-mingled spatially, culturally and intellectually. The public space is "one in which different constructions of religion, and therefore different constructions of secularity, are now bumping up against each other in shared space or shared territory." How we learn to share such territory is therefore the major challenge. This particular respondent predicts that new political affinities and alliances will emerge, made up of "new and strange bed-fellows". These alliances are less likely to be driven by loyalty to traditional ideological positions and political parties, but rather, more by individual intuition. This search for what the contributor calls "a common-life politics" is envisaged as a defining feature of a new post-neoliberal consensus that has been gathering pace since the financial crash of 2008, and which seems to be partially re-expressed in the Brexit vote in 2016 and again in the election of Donald Trump to the US Presidency. A common life politics is thus described as:

> ... different in kind from either multiculturalism or identity politics. The key difference is whether you're willing to contribute to a common life or not. The ticket of entry is not adherence to a prior set of beliefs or ideologies. Rather ... a better indicator of your commitment to the common life is that you actually turn up, you actively contribute to, and you invest as an institution or a tradition in forms of shared life.

Another theological participant suggests that Western popular culture shows the persistent search for a magical or transcendent reality that exists beneath, or is intertwined with, the material and empirical realities of everyday life – referred to as "liquid forms of enchantment". The cultural representations of these existential questions offer important opportunities for public discourse shaped by theological ideas and motifs.

## Religious Studies

In Religious Studies there is a sense of being taken newly seriously and of renewed recognition and visibility, although what that recognition is, and what the response should be, may not yet have come into focus. Responses suggest that Religious Studies has been something of a 'Cinderella' discipline in many institutions (a distant relation, sidelined from the mainstream), but that many universities are now sensing a need to engage with the study of religion, even if they have not yet worked out how or where. There is a sense that Religious Studies is itself recognising that this is being driven by certain newly hard-edged and visible aspects of religion, such as law, radicalisation and the growth of black majority churches, which are making religion – and therefore religious studies – more prominent than they had expected. In many departments, new modules and courses have been appearing, revolving around the theme of 'religion and society'.

Some interviewees noted that this is partly informed by technical dimensions peculiar to higher education, but reflective of neoliberal trends in the wider world. The UK Research Excellence Framework (REF) is one such – a five-yearly assessment of research quality across British universities that emphasises the importance of research with impact. This is seen as driving a focus on the lived and the spatial in the study of religion in particular. Hence, respondents noted a turn to lived religion and experiential learning, located in issues that students can easily recognise. They also drew attention to the risk that this leads to talk confined only to controversies, which they thought could accidentally reproduce negative tropes and a focus on religion as risk.

Religious Studies respondents also sensed that public bodies are realising that religion is an issue for them to take seriously too, and that Religious Studies is challenging the notion that public bodies sit on one side of a secular/sacred divide – or that there even is such a divide. Likewise, nor do religions sit on one side or the other of public and private. These are binaries that Religious Studies thinks are dissolving anyway. This opens up new spaces in which Religious Studies thinks it can have something important to say. There is some concern that this could tip into instrumentalising Religious Studies as a source of mere information (as opposed to deep learning and understanding) about religion in the public sphere. Religious literacy is emerging as one possible dimension of this – how Religious Studies might equip graduates for engagement with a religiously diverse and pervaded world – bringing forward the intellectual and theoretical while being mindful at the same time of how it applies.

There is also a sense of relief that there is a widespread recognition that religion never went away. Crucially for the focus on interdisciplinarity, Religious Studies is looking to other disciplines – especially Sociology of Religion and Social Policy – as it hardens up its questions. Importantly, it was also noted that for the first time other disciplines are also looking to Religious Studies. This raises the question of how these disciplines respond to each other, and whether there will be mutual respect, an important issue after a period when the status of Religious Studies has been in question. How disciplines talk with each other will need seriously working through.

## Social and Public Policy

Social and Public Policy are beginning to be busy on religions and beliefs, although at least two of the interviewees said either that not enough is happening or that it is nothing but trouble. Welfare, violent extremism and cohesion are the three issues that were most apparent. These present themselves in the form of tricky dilemmas that policy-makers have to deal with and that the study of policy can help with – key among them, how to handle visible manifestations of religions and beliefs, especially the hijab. Violent extremism is also an obvious and prominent theme, and this is the case across the interviews and disciplines. In policy contexts there are pressing questions about the extent to which policy is creating or at least complicating a difficult discourse rather than helping. This applies where policy meets law too. Respondents said that they are not at all keen on law in this area because it does not clarify the muddle; it adds to it. They detect a turn away from talk and towards rights that makes it harder to handle.

The question for them is, how can law settle policy questions about religions and beliefs?

More visible plurality is regarded as another key driver, playing out in the policy arena in anxiety and muddle about which approaches to follow and which words to use – multiculturalism, tolerance? There is a perception that these debates have been spilling over into debates about how policy-makers can be helped to understand the contemporary religion they encounter. Religious literacy is much discussed in this context too.

Political questions about religion are also raised in the context of the study of policy – what is the place of the established church if society is multicultural, or at least plural? More broadly, the study of policy is exploring questions about the extent to which we are really secular, or postsecular, or something else? How should the policy-making class think about the categories of religion, belief and the secular? This draws attention once again to the challenge of interdisciplinarity – where are the scholars who can bring Theology, Religious Studies, Sociology, and Social and Public Policy together?

## *Sociology*

Two big narratives emerged in discussions about the Sociology of Religion. First is the problem of the long-term marginalisation of Sociology of Religion from the wider Sociology community, and therefore its relative silence in public debate. One respondent said:

> Our debates about religion happen within the community of Sociology of Religion. This is all very interesting, but who are we talking to? It results in a lack of analytical frameworks within which the commentariat can engage in this. They've no idea what the questions should be. This hasn't changed, but the interest in religion has.

Interviewees said that this paucity of conversation within the academic Sociology of Religion is mirrored in what happens in schools in teaching and learning about religions and beliefs, and they identified an appetite for addressing this.

The other big narrative is about change. This, itself, breaks down in two ways. First, there is interest in what has changed in wider society to make it suddenly interested in religion again. Here the same themes come up again – violence, law and plurality. Some new ones appear too, namely, marketisation and consumerisation of religions and beliefs, in common with other public spheres; the collapse of old political narratives, and meta narratives of other kinds, but including religious ones; and the move online, which is seen as highly democratising and flattening of the sorts of hierarchies that formal religion has previously depended on.

Second, there is interest in how the religions and beliefs landscape itself has changed. This is not just about the facts and figures – plurality, decline and growth – but also about the quality of religions and beliefs. There is a discourse about the deformalisation of religions and beliefs. There is an emphasis on the embodied and lived, and on the material. There is also an interest in religions and beliefs as health and wellbeing, mindfulness and spirit.

This adds up to a stretchier notion of religions and beliefs as including the 'old forms', but also now informal, non-creedal forms, re-jigged expressions of ancient ones, like Wicca and Paganism, and consumerised, fluid ones that are something of a pick-and-mix. Interviewees also draw attention to non-religion (secularism, humanism), and non-religious beliefs, including those as defined in law (for example, environmentalism). This is contrasted with a widespread view of religion as narrow and top-down, still interested in hierarchies, leadership and structures.

To summarise, Sociology of Religion draws attention to three big challenges: (1) re-thinking secularity on the one hand and the real religious landscape on the other, in order to get religions and beliefs right in teaching and learning in schools and universities, and by extension in wider society; (2) raising the profile of Sociology of Religion so that it is not simply talking to itself, which is tactical and strategic; and (3) how to move beyond Habermas to a public sphere that can actively talk about religions and beliefs. This is theoretical and highly academic, and is raised by a number of interviewees across the disciplines.

## Conclusion: Learning to live with liminality

This chapter has laid out the founding principles on which the network was premised. As well as bringing together for the first time an interdisciplinary focus on religion and belief across the Arts and Humanities, the findings of the project reflect a complex and nuanced debate around religion and belief. It is a lived, embodied materiality that shapes and is shaped by the other materialities around it. But it is also a powerful imaginary that intersects and critiques, as well as supports, other political and cultural imaginaries seeking a hegemonic position in the new global order.

This highlights a new set of emerging themes, including the contested role of religion within modern liberal states; the problem of violence that emerges from both religious and secular forms of exceptionalism; the increasing de-sacralisation of the public sphere in politics, culture and education and the struggle of legal and policy frameworks to address new diversities and subjectivities; the growing interest in spaces, landscapes and geographies of religious and spiritual practice and the ways these intersect with new political and civic forms of engagement; the blurring but also hardening of both religious and secular boundaries and identities; new forms of ethical engagement and participation; the need for new understandings of how modernity and religion do coexist and how this shapes public policy; the importance of understanding the nuance and complexity of the secular identity as well as the religious; and the need for a new imagination of the public sphere.

The challenge posed by these findings is both practical and conceptual. At the level of practice it is about how to engage well with the greater secularity, plurality, informality and diversity of religions and beliefs that are being discovered or identified as happening all at once. Tools and approaches are emerging in a variety of disciplines and practices. But this presents a conceptual challenge too: how do these disciplines and practices communicate with each other in ways that can truly inform the future? Religions and beliefs pose a truly interdisciplinary challenge to the old and new disciplines that are increasingly engaging them. A key part of that will be epistemological: in order to engage across the range of intellectual resources and debates it will be necessary to learn how to bridge the classic epistemologies and binaries – science and religion, secular and sacred, private and public, formal and informal. Another is methodological – working out ways of asking questions of and reaching constituencies who are not arrayed around identifiable hierarchies and structures. The real religious landscape no longer looks like that; neither should the landscapes of the disciplines that study it.

An overarching trajectory that contains many of these challenges and tensions is the sense, reflected by all our contributors, that we are clearly emerging out of one paradigm (namely, a neoliberal, materialist one), but it is not yet apparent what the new threshold or paradigm looks like. Thus classically the global order has entered a state of what Victor Turner (1969), drawing on the earlier work of Arnold van Gennep, would call liminality – a disorientating and non-binary space where old certainties and hierarchies are overturned until such a time as a new resolution and clarity of identity is reached. Habermas' (2005, p 25) well-rehearsed call to re-imagine a postsecular public square hints at this; we need to re-imagine the current public square as a space '… in which the vigorous continuation of religion in a continually secularising environment must be reckoned with.' In other words, the public sphere is an increasingly contested and confused space in which both ongoing religion and ongoing secularisation and secularism are taking place, thus profoundly problematising the assumed role of religion as the private other in the publicly neutral space of the secular public sphere. Another commentator of equal authority to Habermas, Charles Taylor (2007, p 711), refers to 'unquiet frontiers' on the borders of modernity. The outcome of 'a secular age', Taylor suggests, has been the consistent stripping out of 'the great languages of transcendence' (2007, p 727). It has been suggested that this has been replaced with a more immanent narrative of individual salvation through consumer culture, albeit often dressed up in 'religious form' (Eagleton, 2014, p 90). Taylor suggests that many people are instinctively dissatisfied with this thin vision of human life and the pressures that are involved in aspiring to it, and are seeking instead various forms of reconnection – what Landy and Saler (2009) describe as a 're-enchantment of the world'. This search spills out into a multitude of personal positions that represent a 'super nova' of possibilities (Taylor, 2007, p 299) that are not likely to be met by old-style authoritarian and institutional religion, but that do not rule out the vicarious influence of such institutions in articulating a vision of a more communitarian and decent society. However, neither Habermas nor Taylor offer a road map out of these liminal spaces. The concept of the postsecular is highly contested, and even the idea that there is another side of the threshold is questioned. Instead, a state of constant change and fluidity becomes the only norm, driven by continuous innovation and globalisation. Manuel Vásquez (2011, p 264) describes this relentless energy and change in a metaphor inspired by Gilles Deleuze: globalisation's relentless dialectic of de-territorialisation and re-territorialisation, he claims, has 'released religion from the constraints of the personal sphere and the container of the secular nation-state.' Woodhead (2012) agrees that the permanent fluidity and accelerated processes of change associated with globalised capitalism have seen religion in the 21st-century West increasingly decoupled from the weakened nation-state and instead ever more aligned to consumer capitalism and the media. She asserts, 'There is no question of a "return" to religion', by which she means a mindset and social order rooted in Christendom, with 'state-like, religious bureaucracies and hierarchies of leadership' (Woodhead, 2012, p 26). But neither is it clear what such a post-Christendom looks like. Instead, Woodhead (2012, p 27) suggests, the present era is one in which 'old certainties were lost and a small number of old gods lost authority and a vast number of new ones arose to take their place.'

At this possibly permanently liminal threshold that constitutes our new global world, what new intellectual spaces are shaping the way in which religions and beliefs are imagined, and what new policy spaces are opening up that help shape the way religion and belief are engaged in the public sphere?

### References

Eagleton, T. (2014) *Culture and the death of God*, New Haven, CT: Yale University Press.

Eder, K. (2006) 'Post-secularism: A return to the public sphere', *Eurozine*, 17 August (www.eurozine.com/post-secularism-a-return-to-the-public-sphere/?pdf).

Habermas, J. (2005) 'Equal treatment of cultures and the limits of postmodern liberalism', *Journal of Political Philosophy*, vol 13, no 1, pp 1-28.

Landy, J. and Saler, M. (2009) *The re-enchantment of the world: Secular magic in a rational world*, Stanford, CA: Stanford University Press.

Taylor, C. (2007) *A secular age*, Cambridge, MA: Harvard University Press.

Turner, V. (1969) *The ritual process: Structure and anti-structure*, Chicago, IL: Aldine.

Vásquez, M. (2011) *More than belief: A materialist theory of religion*, Oxford: Oxford University Press.

Woodhead, L. (2012) 'Introduction', in L. Woodhead and R. Catto (ed) *Religion and change in modern Britain*, London: Routledge, pp 1-33.

# THREE

# Geographical landscapes of religion

Paul Cloke and Andrew Williams

## Introduction

In this chapter we trace the contribution of geographers to the re-imagination of religion and belief. Any claim that Geography has made such a contribution may come as something of a surprise to scholars both outside and inside Geography, given the staunchly secular nature of most geographical endeavour in which acceptance of religion and faith as a legitimate focus for study has been one of the last great areas of otherness that geographers have had to address. For much of its academic history, Human Geography has included a self-contained strand of research about religious spaces (particularly in the US) and in addition has recognised the contributions to wider scholarship from high-profile and self-identifying Christians (such as Lily Kong, David Livingstone and David Ley). More generally, however, the discipline has tended to equate religion with colonising practices of war, violence and proselytisation rather than as a potential contributor to politically progressive or theoretically interesting aspects of space, society and environment.

We identify at least three forms of inquisitiveness that have begun to change this rather skewed pattern. First, from positions outside of

Geography, theologians and philosophers of religion have begun to interrogate geographical concepts in order to pose serious questions about space and place; Kim Knott (2005, 2008), for example, has explored specifically geographical ideas in her accounts of the theorisation of spaces and places of religion, belief and politics, and of the utility of spatial metaphors in religious and political discourse. In so doing, inherently geographical discussions about how places and landscapes are infused with social and cultural meaningfulness have attracted the interest of a wider body of scholars of religion. Second, within Geography, the emergence of religion as a global concern served to catalyse enquiry into religion across a range of sub-disciplines, particularly Political Geography (see, for example, work on religious geopolitics by Agnew, 2006; Dittmer, 2007, 2008; Sturm, 2013; citizenship by Nagel and Staeheli, 2008; and war/peace by Megoran, 2010; P. Williams, 2015), and Social and Cultural Geography, especially with regard to geographies of Islam and Muslim identities (Falah and Nagel, 2005; Gale, 2007; Phillips, 2009), intersectionality (Hopkins et al, 2017) and transnational religious subjectivities, mobilities and politics (Olson and Silvey, 2006; Gökarıksel and Secor, 2009; Sheringham, 2010; Vanderbeck et al, 2011; Ley and Tse, 2013). Much of this work has been animated by postcolonial, queer and feminist theory (Olson et al, 2013a), alongside more longstanding commitments of critical race studies (Gale, 2007), which has brought to the sub-field a critical focus on lived religion, difference and marginality. Third, following the cultural turn in Geography, imaginative conceptual interest in the non-representational (Thrift, 1996, 2007; Anderson and Harrison, 2010) and the more-than-representational (Lorimer, 2005) has paved the way for a recognition of how the world is perpetually re-enacted through practice, including how spiritual practices have the capacity to affect and enchant particular spaces (Holloway, 2003, 2006). Alongside this kind of conceptual experimentation, more orthodox state-centred approaches to governance have been questioned due to the emergence of new forms of ethical citizenship (Cloke, 2002; Cloke et al, 2007, 2012) involving faith-based interventions in care and social justice (Beaumont and Cloke, 2012). Together, the potential place-meaningfulness of spiritual practice, and the contribution of faith-motivation to the formation of spaces of care and justice, have provoked a serious re-engagement with religion within Geography, as evidenced in Stanley Brunn's (2015) five-volume tome of evidence, *The changing world religion map*.

## Geography's longstanding interest in religion

As Brunn's compilation illustrates, the longstanding bedrock of Geography's engagement with religion has involved attempts to understand how sacred spaces and religious landscapes are constructed, perceived and experienced (see, for example, Park, 1994). As Olson et al (2013a) have documented, 'geographies of religion' have developed trademark ideas and metaphors to present socio-spatial and cultural understandings of the sacred. Thus, the notion of 'sacred spaces' has been used to investigate the private, 'behind-closed-doors' geographies of religious buildings and meeting places, and in particular has prompted questions about the symbolic meaningfulness therein (see Jackson and Henrie, 1983). Similarly, ideas about 'sacred landscapes' have been deployed to suggest how cultural landscapes become depicted and characterised according to different forms of religion and belief (see Lane, 2002), and how the social mobilities of pilgrimage add further meaning to sites and routes (see Stoddart and Morinis, 1997).

Although these longstanding interests are often expressed as historic phenomena, their geographies rarely stand still, and the study of religion by geographers is marked in particular by a series of attempts to account for the complex interrelations between religion, migration and multiculturalism. Thus attention to sacred landscapes has come to include accounts of how particular cities have become characterised by the dynamic demographics of religious identity and by the emergence of new kinds of formal sacred spaces (see Nayak, 2012; Dwyer et al, 2016). Accordingly, Kong (2001) identifies a set of new religious geographies focusing both on different sites of religious practice and on the wider implications of particular religious practices in place-specific contexts. Geographies of religion have therefore begun to embrace not only a wider range of formal sacred spaces than previously recognised, but also the increased relevance of more unofficial sites of religious involvement – bookshops, tourism, cultural and artistic spaces, welfare provision, protests and the like – suggesting to some commentators a complex process of de-sacralising and re-sacralising of religious impacts on urban and other landscapes.

Overall, these longstanding interests of geographies of religion have proved to be more successful in contextualising religious belief in an infrastructure of spaces and landscapes than in presenting a credible case for attending to religion as an integral part of the mainstream of geographical focus. Despite potential synergy with crucial demographic and cultural trends, particularly in cities, these orthodox concerns have tended, by and large, to uphold a freestanding Geography of Religion rather than a fully integrated and widely accepted immersion of religion into the core issues of Geography, although as noted earlier this is starting to change in some quarters. As Olson et al (2013b) conclude, it is only when overly safe and uncritical assumptions about what is sacred and what is secular are challenged by geographers that a more complex and widely acceptable account of how religion is spatialised and socialised can be advanced. Our intention in this chapter is not to provide a comprehensive overview of the ongoing development of geographies of religion (see Kong, 1990, 2001, 2010; Holloway and Valins, 2002; Olson and Silvey, 2006; Stump, 2008; Brace et al, 2011; Hopkins et al, 2013). Instead, in the remainder of this chapter we discuss three rather different forms of religious landscapes that have emerged from the challenge to the longstanding binaries of sacred and secular, in which attention to how spaces and landscapes are performed opens up more complex, dynamic and often hybrid spaces and subjectivities relating to religion.

## Lived religious landscapes

Geographical approaches to lived religion focus on how individuals construct, negotiate, perform, experience and contest religious spaces, beliefs and practices. Hopkins et al (2011) provide us with an excellent series of narratives about the importance of 'lived religion' in which the emphasis is on how places are both scripted and narrated in and through the lives of faith-motivated people and organisations. Their approach (see in particular Olson et al, 2013b) is founded on the recognition of a number of deliberate intersections between religious practice and mainstream theoretical development in the Social Sciences. Thus, from postcolonial theory they recognise the importance of the religious gaze in the shaping of social order and in the deployment of myths that instruct about how religion should be lived out. Attention to the presence and operation of such a gaze is fundamental in reaching an understanding of how religious landscapes are constructed and maintained. Equally, they use aspects of feminist theory to emphasise how the embodied lives of faith-motivated people and groups are crucial to an understanding of how religious identities are made complex in their formation and negotiation. For example, the expression of religiosity by women is inevitably intersected with other aspects of identity, for example, ethnicity and sexuality, as well as by the often-dominant expressions of masculinity that pervade religious regulation (see also Hopkins, 2006; Dwyer et al, 2008; Ehrkamp, 2008). To these theoretical inputs we can add elements of poststructural thinking that allow for reflexive attention to the transcendent. Sutherland's (2017) notion of 'theography' helps to produce more nuanced understandings of the religious subject by exploring the kinds of reflexivity that direct subjects towards struggles over the content of theology, as well as to its effects on their spatial imagination, and their praxis. Theography ties together poststructural ideas about the potential of the religious subject to subvert abstract categorisation with lived geographies that are formed by the subject's reframing of theology in situations where practical settings are made sense of in and through particular understandings of transcendence. In this way, lived religion arises from a mix of having a theological map and the variable usefulness of that map in the multiple contexts and situations of ordinary life.

Each of these theoretical reflections is able to contribute to the task of providing a more nuanced understanding of how the complex spaces and subjectivities of religion are lived out in the everyday practice of ordinary life. The significance of lived religious landscapes is evidenced in a series of studies by geographers, illustrating, for example, the everyday lives of being a young Christian person in Glasgow (Vincett et al, 2012), the complex constraints and freedoms experienced by young British Muslim women (Dwyer, 1999; Hopkins and Gale, 2009) and the everyday disillusionment that can occur among faith-motivated activists when inward-looking religious institutions fail to address key ethical issues of community care or social and environmental justice (Cloke and Pears, 2016). This emphasis on the embodied living of religious landscapes is a significant development in geographies of religion, not least because it offers tangible understandings of how ordinary religious identities become part of broader places and spaces, how ordinary religious affiliation and identity are active in positioning individuals and communities in the issues and politics of the public square, and how blocky categorisations are inadequate to capture the complexity of lived religious identities. Foregrounding the contested spaces and practices of lived religion has also helped geographers of religion offer more nuanced readings of a wide-ranging set of phenomena, including the spatialities of spiritual experience (Wigley, 2017), Islamophobia and misrecognition (Hopkins et al, 2017), as well as offering spatial perspectives on the politics and ethics of religious conversion (Woods, 2012; Kong and Nair, 2014; Williams, in press).

## Spiritual landscapes

A second emergent strand within contemporary geographies of religion draws on ideas from non-representational theory and psychogeographical research in order to take seriously religion's claim to be associated with and involved in transcendence. The idea of 'spiritual landscapes' (Dewsbury and Cloke, 2009) uses concepts from post-phenomenology to tease out how landscape (existence), practice (performance) and affect (immanence) offer up alternative ways to understand how faith and belief and phenomenology recast our notion of being in the world. As such it attempts to understand particular spaces and landscapes in terms of the experiential surplus, or excess, of the spiritual – what Wilford (2012) has termed the 'more than' of religion. In this way, alongside an appreciation of that which is tangible and known about in the local and global worlds of religion, it is argued that we need to embrace elements of the non-rational – the other-worldly – to grasp fully the geographies of religion. To do so, geographers have recognised the need to embrace the immaterial push of spirit alongside the materiality of landscape by rendering spiritual landscapes as the associate mapping of the relations between bodily existence, felt practice and faith in something immanent but not manifest as such. The importance and centrality of the spiritual landscapes is that they have a capacity to forge a sense of community, which can become a recognisable part of individual and communal disposition.

Attention to spiritual landscapes, then, invites geographies of religion to reach out beyond material and representational landscapes of society, economy, politics and culture, and to acknowledge that practice is also co-constructed in a spiritual register. This conceptual grasp of the spiritual involves an openness to being affected by something other than the material present world – something found in the performative presences (and absences) of some sense of spirit. It has been advanced more generally in Geography to identify both the dream-like and ghost-like phantasmagorias of everyday life (Pile, 2005), and more specifically to identify the importance of new forms of spirituality (MacKian, 2012; Bartolini et al, 2017a). Bartolini et al (2017b), for example, examine the mediation of affects and bodies in Spirit communication within Spiritualist churches in Stoke-on-Trent. Seeking to move beyond categorisations of Spiritualism as enchanted, extraordinary or simply the entertaining theatrics of the spirit medium, they draw attention to the evidential procedures and affective relays between the medium, the message receiver and the congregation that render talking to the dead ordinary and mundane. Spiritualism, they argue, works not through the overt management of affect, but through the undecidability and indeterminacy of emergent affects and whether they feel right or not. Bartolini et al (2017b) provide an insightful examination of the spatial processes at work in the success – or not – of spirit communication, and more broadly, the place of spirit in the everyday lives of Spiritualists.

In a similar vein, Williams' (2016) residential ethnographic work inside a Christian therapeutic community working with people in alcohol and drug recovery explored the performativity of Pentecostal practices of worship. It highlighted the viscerally felt manifestations of the Holy Spirit, and how these embodied sensations came to be coded and interpreted through the canonical language of the community. Acknowledging the micropolitics of religious practice, including the material and discursive staging of worship space as well as the participatory manners of Pentecostal worship, the study also considered the therapeutic possibilities attached to, and derived from, engagements with the Spirit. Several residents documented powerful encounters with divine presences, understood through felt somatic experience (heat, tingling, peace, joy, ecstasy), which came to reaffirm existing, and generate new, transformations in self-identity and religious belief. Assent to belief, however, is no guarantee of spiritual experience, as shown in religious and non-religious residents feeling 'disconnected' and alienated from the event-space of worship. It is important, therefore, for analysis of spiritual landscapes to acknowledge both the inherent indeterminacy and the complex relationalities between bodies, ethical proclivities and materialities involved in the presencing of other-worldly spirits.

More significantly, however, spiritual landscapes also provide geographies of religion with the opportunity to make stronger connections with different strands of theological scholarship. For example, Volf's (2013) exposition of how to practice *A public faith* encourages ways of seeking the public good as a third way between resorting to religious violence and isolation in a religious cultural ghetto. This search, he insists, involves constantly iterating practices of ascending to God in order to receive and discern prophetic messages, and returning to the world to practice the received messages in among mundane daily life. Aside from the metaphorical ascent and descent of this message, Volf's picture of religious practice suggests a sense of closely interrelated materiality and spirituality in everyday life that reinforces the need to understand the spiritual landscapes in which particular places and spaces are set. Equally, acknowledgement of spiritual landscapes enables geographers to take seriously Wink's (1992) assertion that the powers of evil work simultaneously as an outer visible structure and as an inner spiritual reality, and that the need to recognise real spiritual forces that emanate from real institutions and real systems of domination is fundamental to any understanding of geographies of evil (Cloke, 2011a). As with Volf's use of the idea of ascending–descending, the binary inside–outside metaphor in Wink's account is less important than the recognition of an experiential surplus – a spiritual excess – that transcends the material geographies of religion.

One interesting dynamic of these spiritual landscapes is the capacity to affect people and communities with a directed performative force. A useful example of such a force is presented by Holloway (2013) in his account of how an ethos of engagement with theological and faithful sensibilities can affect a patterning of qualitative intensity that results in atmospheres of hopefulness. By and large, geographers have regarded hope as a rather weak concept when compared, for example, to ideas about democracy, social justice and political resistance (see, for example, Sparke, 2008). However, in the context of spiritual landscapes, hope can represent an unseen yet powerful force that affects those who practice it and those who are formed through its event. Hope, of course, need not be spiritual (Anderson, 2006), but Holloway asserts a spiritual brand of hope that has the capacity to produce an ethos, a disposition, that affects and is affected by the hope of something better. In some places, such hopefulness can be key to understanding the emotional dynamics of place. For example, in her narrative of everyday practice in the city of Christchurch, New Zealand, following the destructive earthquakes in 2010 and 2011, Parsons (2014) demonstrates that both religious and secular elements of the city's population were affected by both a lack of hope and a search for hope. The resultant emotional landscapes were patterned by processes of lament, care, cultural experimentation and renewal in which religion played a significant part.

## Landscapes of postsecularity

A third emergent strand in geographies of religion is marked by the critical engagement of human geographers with ideas concerning the blurring of the sacred and the secular and with the conceptual potential for geographies of postsecularity. Despite widespread scepticism from the majority of social scientists about the veracity and utility of any supposed postsecular turn, some human geographers have been fascinated by empirical evidence that seems in some ways to support Eder's (2006) observation that the hushed-up voice of religion in the public sphere is beginning to be heard again, and Habermas' (2010) recognition of the postsecular as a repository of the progressive democratic values that can emerge when the sum of religious and secular reasoning becomes more than its constituent parts. Research has charted the increasingly high-profile role of faith-based organisations (Beaumont and Cloke, 2012; Cloke et al, 2013) in these arenas, and although it is certainly the case that many such activities take place within religious–secular divides, these activities have actively created new spaces of care, welfare and protest against poverty and social marginalisation, and more broadly against austerity governance and neoliberalised capitalism. Although there is clear evidence of longstanding faith-based activity in some of these areas, there seems to have been a surge of faith-based involvement from the 1980s onward, at least in part as a context-contingent response to social problems in the 'mean times' (Cloke et al, 2017). Moreover, recent studies (Beaumont and Baker, 2011; Cloke and Beaumont, 2012; A. Williams, 2015; Cloke et al, 2016) offer evidence that a significant dynamic within this emerging political environment is the rise in postsecular partnerships (or rapprochements; see Cloke, 2011b) of care and advocacy that work across religious–secular divides. In some cases it is suggested that these spaces of postsecularity have not only disturbed boundaries between the religious and the secular, but have also opened up alternative imaginaries and practices with a capacity to generate the possibility for new kinds of ethical spaces and subjectivities.

Postsecularity, if treated with conceptual respect and humility, provides fertile ground for new kinds of approaches to geographies of religion. These issues of respect and humility are crucial. For many, the very idea of the postsecular is utterly unpalatable, representing an oversimplified and yet overblown rewriting of history that misunderstands secularisation while seeking to reify the social contribution of religion (see, for example, Kong, 2010; Wilford, 2010; Ley, 2011; Beckford, 2012). Such critique is energised by all-too-sweeping descriptions of a supposedly 'postsecular age', 'postsecular city' or 'postsecular public sphere'. However, it is much more difficult to deny the emergence of particular sites, spaces and practices of postsecularity bubbling up within the city and the public sphere. This more modest proposition represents for us a more accurate reflection of the geographies involved, and it is in this bubbling up of postsecularity that human geographers have begun to base their claims about the appearance of new forms of ethicality – both in terms of spaces and of subjectivities – in which particular postsecular technologies can be seen to be at work. Such work builds on poststructural and feminist contributions to ethics (Popke, 2003; Braidotti, 2006) to challenge liberal visions of the subject as the moral agent and instead emphasise the relationalities that shape the process of becoming ethical subjects. The focus on ethicality foregrounds analysis on the spaces, technologies and contested politics through which ethical sensibilities are made, (un)made and (re)made, and crucially, the ways in which ethical subjectivities connect to political mobilisation. Read in this way, postsecularity provides a conceptual tool to discern how subjectivities are formed in and through neoliberal logics in late-capitalist societies, as well as more hopeful and insurgent ethical sensibilities that can emerge through religious and secular collaboration. Postsecularity is commonly found in the interstices of austere neoliberalised governance, where faith-based groups seem to be finding particular crossover narratives with which to work together with secular and other religious parties, leading sometimes to partnerships in which there is some reflexive translation involving mutual understanding and appreciation that results in assimilated practice. A range of examples of these practices is detailed in a new book, *Geographies of postsecularity* (Baker et al, in press).

In some ways, discussion of the progressive potential of spaces and subjectivities of postsecularity poses a threat to orthodox and longstanding interests in the geography of religion, not least in terms of a fear that religious concepts in postsecular contexts are inevitably diluted, deradicalised and assimilated into the secular mainstream. However, human geographers have begun to demonstrate the opposite effect, wherein religious concepts, and the theo-ethical (Cloke et al, 2007; Cloke, 2010, 2011) precepts that underlie them, are becoming re-connected to their societal roots as part of a technology of postsecularity that takes religion seriously. It is important to emphasise in this context that emergent spaces of postsecularity can be regressive as well as progressive. Collusion between fundamentalist religion and conservative political factions has been shown not only to form partnerships that sell their soul to neoliberalised austerity in faith-based outbursts of malignant neglect of the socially and economically marginalised (Hackworth, 2012), but also to give rise to social and political movements that offer frenzied and violent hatred towards others, especially in areas of sexuality and gender rights (Bruce, 2017). However, this 'dark side' of landscapes of postsecularity should not be permitted to overshadow the politically progressive potential and ethical capacity of landscapes of postsecularity in which care for the marginalised and justice for the oppressed are theo-ethically ingrained in rapprochements aiming to resist neoliberal austerity and provide compassion and material succour to its victims.

## Conclusion

This chapter has outlined the contours of three forms of religious landscape, each offering human geographers and those beyond the discipline a set of new conceptual tools and empirical concerns. As geographies of religion continue to develop as a vibrant sub-field in Human Geography, we wish to echo arguments made by Olson et al (2013a) and others (Kong, 2010; Dwyer, 2016) for greater recognition of what geographical perspectives on religion, spirituality and belief might offer. While geographical scholarship has established a critical focus on the intersections of space, scale, place and religion, we suggest that geographical approaches offer more than an analytical framework or spatial vocabulary through which to study the field of religion and belief. In this chapter we have highlighted a series of geographic engagements with religious landscapes that represent a marked shift beyond the 'modernist academic gaze, which ignored or suppressed the agency and salience of the sacred, in favour of approaches which include the religious and the spiritual in frameworks of analysis and explanation' (Dwyer, 2016, p 758). Indeed, the theoretical turn to more-than-representational and post-phenomenological approaches has revitalised geographical agendas on religion by providing a set of conceptual frameworks that invite critical re-examination of traditional spaces of geographical enquiry, including the performativity of sacred spaces, pilgrimage and religious experience (Finlayson, 2012, 2017; Finlayson and Mesev, 2013; Foley, 2013; Maddrell and della Dora, 2013; Wade and Hynes 2013; Scriven, 2014). Geographical scholarship is only recently taking seriously Holloway's (2013, p 204) call to give more analytical space 'to those extraordinary forces that the faithful will always say move them to action.' Such a move invariably raises a series of ontological and epistemological challenges (Dwyer, 2016; Bartolini et al, 2017b), and the claim here is not to categorically affirm the existence of a deity or the supernatural but rather to offer geographical accounts that are faithful to the spiritual ontologies that 'co-constitute the material, bodily, sensational and sensory worlds of religious subjectivities' (Williams, 2016, p 47). Geographic analysis of spiritual landscapes provides new insight into lived religious landscapes, illustrating the dynamic spaces and practices through which traditional notions of 'the sacred' and 'the secular' become unstable, fluid and contested. Spiritual landscapes also offer important insights into the formation of hybrid spaces and subjectivities of postsecularity, revealing the shifting terrain of religious and secular enchantment in contemporary politics and public realm, and the spiritual excesses of hope and reciprocity that make possible new forms of ethicality.

Moving ahead, geographical scholarship on religion and belief must pursue these theoretical and empirical avenues while retaining its critical foci on space, politics, difference and marginality, and on how lived religious landscapes intersect with class, ethnicity, sexuality, age and subculture. Thus far, the bulk of scholarship has predominantly focused on monotheistic religions (notable exceptions include Mawdsley, 2006; McConnell, 2013; Hopkins et al, 2017; Qian and Kong, 2017). Alongside this focus, much greater attention also needs to be given to indigenous religious and spiritual traditions, including serious study of the place of magic, witchcraft and spiritual ontologies in development geography and environmental management (Smith, 2017), and to aspects of non-religion and non-belief.

## References

Agnew, J. (2006) 'Religion and geopolitics', *Geopolitics*, vol 11, no 2, pp 183-91.

Anderson, B. (2006) '"Transcending without transcendence": Utopianism and an ethos of hope', *Antipode*, vol 38, no 4, pp 691-710.

Anderson, B. and Harrison, P. (eds) (2010) *Taking-place: Non-representational theories and geography*, Farnham: Ashgate.

Baker, C., Cloke, P., Sutherland, C. and Williams, A. (in press) *Geographies of postsecularity: Re-envisioning politics, subjectivity and ethics*, London: Routledge.

Bartolini, N., MacKian, S. and Pile, S. (2017b) 'Talking with the dead: Spirit mediumship, affect and embodiment in Stoke-on-Trent', *Transactions of the Institute of British Geographers*, doi:10.1111/tran.12207.

Bartolini, N., Chris, R., MacKian, S. and Pile, S. (2017a) 'The place of spirit: Modernity and the geographies of spirituality', *Progress in Human Geography*, vol 41, no 3, pp 338-54.

Beaumont, J. and Baker, C. (eds) (2011) *Postsecular cities: Space, theory and practice*, London: Continuum.

Beaumont, J. and Cloke, P. (eds) (2012) *Faith-based organisations and exclusion in European cities*, Bristol: Policy Press.

Beckford, J. (2012) 'SSSR presidential address. Public religions and the postsecular: Critical reflections', *Journal for the Scientific Study of Religion*, vol 51, no 1, pp 1-19.

Brace, C., Bailey, A., Carter, S., Harvey, D. and Thomas, N. (eds) (2011) *Emerging geographies of belief*, Newcastle upon Tyne: Cambridge Scholars.

Braidotti, R. (2006) *Transpositions: On nomadic ethics*, Cambridge: Polity Press

Bruce, S. (2017) *Politics and religion*, Cambridge: Polity Press.

Brunn, S. (ed) (2015) *The changing world religion map: Sacred places, identities, practices and politics*, Netherlands: Springer.

Cloke, P. (2002) 'Deliver us from evil? Prospects for living ethically and acting politically in human geography', *Progress in Human Geography*, vol 26, no 5, pp 587-604.

Cloke, P. (2010) 'Theo-ethics and radical faith-based praxis in the postsecular city', in A. Molendijk, J. Beaumont and C. Jedan (eds) *Exploring the postsecular: The religious, the political and the urban*, Leiden: Brill, pp 223-41.

Cloke, P. (2011a) 'Emerging geographies of evil? Theo-ethics and postsecular possibilities', *Cultural Geographies*, vol 18, no 4, pp 475-93.

Cloke, P. (2011b) 'Emerging postsecular rapprochement in the contemporary city', in J. Beaumont and C. Baker (eds) *Postsecular cities: Space, theory and practice*, London: Continuum, pp 237-54.

Cloke, P. and Beaumont, J. (2013) 'Geographies of postsecular rapprochement in the city', *Progress in Human Geography*, vol 37, no 1, pp 27-51.

Cloke, P. and Pears, M. (eds) (2016) *Mission in marginal places: The praxis*, Milton Keynes: Paternoster Press.

Cloke, P., Beaumont, J. and Williams, A. (eds) (2013) *Working faith: Faith-based organisations and urban social justice*, Milton Keynes: Paternoster Press.

Cloke, P., May, J. and Johnsen, S. (2007) 'Ethical citizenship? Volunteers and the ethics of providing services for homeless people', *Geoforum*, vol 38 no 6, pp 1089-101.

Cloke, P., May, J. and Williams, A. (2017) 'The geographies of food banks in the meantime', *Progress in Human Geography*, vol 41, no 6, pp 703-26.

Cloke, P., Sutherland, C. and Williams, A. (2016) 'Postsecularity, political resistance, and protest in the Occupy Movement', *Antipode*, vol 48, no 3, pp 497-523.

Dewsbury, J.D. and Cloke P. (2009) 'Spiritual landscapes: Existence, performance and immanence', *Social and Cultural Geography*, vol 10, no 6, pp 695-711.

Dittmer, J. (2007) 'Intervention: Religious geopolitics', *Political Geography*, vol 26, no 7, pp 737-9.

Dittmer, J. (2008) 'The geographical pivot of (the end of) history: Evangelical geopolitical imaginations and audience interpretation of left behind', *Political Geography*, vol 27, no 3, pp 280-300.

Dwyer, C. (1999) 'Veiled meanings: Young British Muslim women and the negotiation of differences', *Gender, Place and Culture: A Journal of Feminist Geography*, vol 6, no 1, pp 5-26.

Dwyer, C. (2016) 'Why does religion matter for cultural geographers?', *Social & Cultural Geography*, vol 17, no 6, pp 758-62.

Dwyer, C., Shah, B. and Sanghera, G. (2008) '"From cricket lover to terror suspect": Challenging representations of young British Muslim men', *Gender, Place and Culture: A Journal of Feminist Geography*, vol 15, no 2, pp 117-36.

Dwyer, C., Tse, J. and Ley, D. (2016) '"Highway to heaven": The creation of a multicultural, religious landscape in suburban Richmond, British Columbia', *Social and Cultural Geography*, vol 17, no 5, pp 667-93.

Eder, K. (2006) 'Post-secularism: A return to the public sphere', *Eurozine*, 17 August (www.eurozine.com/post-secularism-a-return-to-the-public-sphere/?pdf).

Ehrkamp, P. (2008) 'Risking publicity: Masculinities and the racialization of public neighborhood space', *Social and Cultural Geography*, vol 9, no 2, pp 117-33.

Falah, G.W and Nagel, C (eds) (2005) *Geographies of Muslim women: Gender, religion, and space*, New York: Guildford.

Finlayson, C. (2012) 'Spaces of faith: Incorporating emotion and spirituality in geographic studies', *Environment and Planning A*, vol 44, no 7, pp 1763-78.

Finlayson, C. (2017) 'Church-in-a-box: Making space sacred in a non-traditional setting', *Journal of Cultural Geography*, vol 34, no 3, pp 303-23.

Finlayson, C. and Mesev, V. (2013) 'Emotional encounters in sacred spaces: The case of the Church of Jesus Christ of Latter-day Saints', *The Professional Geographer*, vol 66, no 3, pp 436-42.

Foley, R. (2013) 'Small health pilgrimages: Place and practice at the holy well', *Culture and Religion*, vol 14, no 1, pp 44-62.

Gale, R. (2007) 'The place of Islam in the geography of religion: Trends and intersections', *Geography Compass*, vol 1, no 5, pp 1015-36.

Gökarıksel, B. and Secor, A.J. (2009) 'New transnational geographies of Islamism, capitalism, and subjectivity: The veiling-fashion industry in Turkey', *Area*, vol 41, no 1, pp 6-18.

Habermas, J. (2010) *An awareness of what is missing: Faith and reason in a post-secular age*, Cambridge: Polity Press.

Hackworth, J. (2012) *Faith-based: Religious neoliberalism and the politics of welfare in the United States*, Athens, GA: University of Georgia Press.

Holloway, J. (2003) 'Make-believe: Spiritual practice, embodiment and sacred space', *Environment and Planning A*, vol 35, no 11, pp 1961-74.

Holloway, J. (2006) 'Enchanted spaces: The séance, affect, and geographies of religion', *Annals of the Association of American Geographers*, vol 96, no 1, pp 182-7.

Holloway, J. (2013) 'The space that faith makes: Towards a (hopeful) ethos of engagement', in L. Kong, P. Hopkins and E. Olson (eds) *Religion and place: Landscape, politics, and piety*, New York: Springer, pp 203-18.

Holloway, J. and Valins, O. (2002) 'Editorial: Placing religion and spirituality in geography', *Social and Cultural Geography*, vol 3, no 1, pp 5-9.

Hopkins, P. (2006) 'Youthful Muslim masculinities: Gender and generational relations', *Transactions of the Institute of British Geographers*, vol 31, no 3, pp 337-52.

Hopkins, P. and Gale, R. (2009) *Muslims in Britain: Race, place and identities*, Edinburgh: Edinburgh University Press.

Hopkins, P., Kong, L. and Olson, E. (eds) (2013) *Religion and place: Landscape, politics and piety*, London: Springer.

Hopkins, P., Botterill, K., Sanghera, G. and Arshad, R. (2017) 'Encountering misrecognition: Being mistaken for being Muslim', *Annals of the American Association of Geographers*, vol 107, no 4, pp 934-48.

Hopkins, P., Olson, E., Pain, R. and Vincett, G. (2011) 'Mapping intergenerationalities: The formation of youthful religiosities', *Transactions of the Institute of British Geographers*, vol 36, no 2, pp 314-27.

Jackson, R. and Henrie, R. (1983) 'Perception of sacred space', *Journal of Cultural Geography*, vol 3, no 2, pp 94-107.

Knott, K. (2005) *The location of religion: A spatial analysis*, London: Oakville.

Knott, K. (2008) 'Spatial theory for the study of religion', *Religion Compass*, vol 2, no 6, pp 1102-16.

Kong, L. (1990) 'Geography and religion: Trends and prospects', *Progress in Human Geography*, vol 14, no 3, pp 355-71.

Kong, L. (2001) 'Mapping "new" geographies of religion: Politics and poetics in modernity', *Progress in Human Geography*, vol 25, no 2, pp 211-33.

Kong, L. (2010) 'Global shifts, theoretical shifts: Changing geographies of religion', *Progress in Human Geography*, vol 34, no 6, pp 755-76.

Kong, L. and Nair, S. (2014) 'Geographies of religious conversion', in L. Rambo and C Farhadian (eds) *The Oxford handbook of religious conversion*, Oxford: Oxford University Press, pp 65-83.

Lane, B. (2002) *Landscapes of the sacred: Geography and narrative in American spirituality*: Baltimore, MD: Johns Hopkins University Press.

Ley, D. (2011) 'Preface', in J. Beaumont and C Baker (eds) *Postsecular cities: Religious space, theory and practice*, London: Continuum, pp xii-xiv.

Ley, D. and Tse, J.K.H. (2013) 'Homo religious? Religion and immigrant subjectivities', in L. Kong, P. Hopkins and E. Olson (eds) *Religion and place: Landscape, politics, and piety*, New York: Springer, pp 149-65.

Lorimer, H. (2005) 'Cultural geography: The busyness of being "more-than-representational"', *Progress in Human Geography*, vol 29, no 1, pp 83-94.

MacKian, S. (2012) *Everyday spirituality: Social and spatial worlds of enchantment*, Basingstoke: Palgrave Macmillan.

Maddrell, A. and della Dora, V. (2013) 'Crossing surfaces in search of the Holy: Landscape and liminality in contemporary Christian pilgrimage', *Environment and Planning A*, vol 45, no 5, pp 1105-26.

Mawdsley, E. (2006) 'Hindu nationalism, neo-traditionalism and environmental discourses in India', *Geoforum*, vol 37, no 3, pp 380-90.

McConnell, F. (2013) 'The geopolitics of Buddhist reincarnation: Contested futures of Tibetan leadership', *Area*, vol 45, no 2, pp 162-9.

Megoran, N. (2010) 'Towards a geography of peace: Pacific geopolitics and evangelical Christian Crusade apologies', *Transactions of the Institute of British Geographers*, vol 35, no 3, pp 382-98.

Nagel, C.R and Staeheli L.A (2008) 'Integration and the negotiation and "Here" and "There": The case of British Arab activists', *Social and Cultural Geography*, vol 9, no 4, pp 415-30.

Nayak, A. (2012) 'Race, religion and British multiculturalism: The political responses of black and minority ethnic voluntary organisations to multicultural cohesion', *Political Geography*, vol 31, no 7, pp 454-63.

Olson, E. and Silvey, R. (2006) 'Transnational geographies: Rescaling development, migration, and religion', *Environment and Planning A*, vol 38, no 5, pp 805-8.

Olson, E., Hopkins, P. and Kong, L. (2013a) 'Introduction. Religion and place: Landscape, politics and piety', in P. Hopkins, L. Kong and E. Olson (eds) *Religion and place: Landscape, politics and piety*, London: Springer, pp 1-20.

Olson, E., Hopkins, P., Pain, R. and Vincett, G. (2013b) 'Retheorizing the postsecular present: Embodiment, spatial transcendence, and challenges to authenticity among young Christians in Glasgow, Scotland', *Annals of the Association of American Geographers*, vol 103, no 6, pp 1421-36.

Park, C. (1994) *Sacred worlds: Introduction to geography and religion*, London: Routledge.

Parsons, M. (2014) *Rubble to resurrection: Churches respond in the Canterbury quakes*, Auckland, New Zealand: Daystar.

Phillips, R. (ed) (2009) *Muslim spaces of hope: Geographies of possibility in Britain and the west*, London: Zed Books.

Pile, S. (2005) *Real cities: Modernity, space and the phantasmagorias of city life*, London: Sage.

Popke, E.J. (2003) 'Poststructuralist ethics: Subjectivity, responsibility and the space of community', *Progress in Human Geography*, vol 27, no 3, pp 298-316.

Qian, J. and Kong, L. (2017) 'Buddhism Co Ltd? Epistemology of religiosity, and the re-invention of a Buddhist monastery in Hong Kong', *Environment and Planning D*, doi.org/10.1177/0263775817733268.

Scriven, R. (2014) 'Geographies of pilgrimage: Meaningful movements and embodied mobilities', *Geography Compass*, vol 8, no 4, pp 249-61.

Sheringham, O. (2010) 'Creating "alternative geographies": Religion, transnationalism and everyday life', *Geography Compass*, vol 4, no 11, pp 1678-94.

Smith, T. (2017) 'Witchcraft, spiritual worldviews and environmental management: Rationality and assemblage', *Environment and Planning A*, vol 49, no 3, pp 592-611.

Sparke, M. (2008) 'Political geography: Political geographies of globalization III: Resistance', *Progress in Human Geography*, vol 32, no 3, pp 423-40.

Stoddart, R. and Morinis, A. (eds) (1997) *Sacred places, sacred spaces: The geography of pilgrimages*, Baton Rouge, LA: Louisiana State University Geoscience Publications.

Stump, R. (2008) *The geography of religion: Faith, place, and space*, Lanham, MD: Rowman & Littlefield.

Sturm, T. (2013) 'The future of religious geopolitics: Towards a research and theory agenda', *Area*, vol 45, no 2, pp 134-40.

Sutherland, C. (2017) 'Theography: Subject, theology, and praxis in geographies of religion', *Progress in Human Geography*, vol 41, no 3, pp 321-37.

Thrift, N. (1996) *Spatial formations*, London: Sage Publications.

Thrift, N. (2007) *Non-representational theory: Space, politics, affect*, London: Routledge.

Vanderbeck, R.M., Andersson, J., Valentine, G., Sadgrove, J. and Ward, K. (2011) 'Sexuality, activism, and witness in the Anglican Communion: The 2008 Lambeth Conference of Anglican Bishops', *Annals of the Association of American Geographers*, vol 101, no 3, pp 670-89.

Vincett, G., Olson, E., Hopkins, P. and Pain, R. (2012) 'Young people and performance: Christianity in Scotland', *Journal of Contemporary Religion*, vol 27, no 2, pp 275-90.

Volf, M. (2013) *A public faith: How followers of Christ should serve the common good* (reprint edn), Grand Rapids, MI: Brazos Press.

Wade, M. and Hynes, M. (2013) 'Worshipping bodies: Affective labour in the Hillsong Church', *Geographical Research*, vol 51, no 2, pp 173-9.

Wigley, E. (2017) 'Constructing subjective spiritual geographies in everyday mobilities: The practice of prayer and meditation in corporeal travel', *Social and Cultural Geography*, doi:10.1080/14649365.2017.1328527.

Wilford, J. (2010) 'Sacred archipelagos: Geographies of secularization', *Progress in Human Geography*, vol 34, no 3, pp 328-48.

Wilford, J. (2012) *Sacred subdivisions: The postsuburban transformation of American evangelicalism*, New York: New York University Press.

Williams, A. (2015) 'Postsecular geographies: Theo-ethics, rapprochement and neoliberal governance in a faith-based drug programme', *Transactions of the Institute of British Geographers*, vol 40, no 2, pp 192-208.

Williams, A. (2016) 'Spiritual landscapes of Pentecostal worship, belief, and embodiment in a therapeutic community: New critical perspectives', *Emotion, Space and Society*, vol 19, pp 45-55.

Williams, A. (in press) 'Lived religion, worship and conversion: Ethnographic reflections in an abstinence-based Christian therapeutic community', in S. Sremac and I. Jindra I (eds) *Conversion and lived religion: Recovery, imprisonment and homelessness*, Leiden: Brill.

Williams, P. (2015) *Everyday peace? Politics, citizenship and Muslim lives in India*, Chichester: Wiley-Blackwell.

Wink, W. (1992) *Engaging the powers: Discernment and resistance in a world of domination*, Minneapolis, MN: Fortress Press.

Woods, O. (2012) 'The geographies of religious conversion', *Progress in Human Geography*, vol 36, no 4, pp 440-56.

# FOUR

# 'Spatial methodology' in religion and belief research: The example of a study of Twelver Shii Muslim networks in Britain

Oliver Scharbrodt

## Introduction

This chapter discusses recent debates on the development of a spatial methodology in the study of diasporic religions and its use in research on minority religious communities, their transnational dimensions and their place and role in public life. These contributions are used to understand the multiple spatial layers in which transnational religious networks are located, and to question some of the discursive dichotomies created around diasporic religious communities such as regressive vs progressive, purity vs hybridity, continuity vs discontinuity and transnationalism vs localism. To exemplify and apply these theoretical reflections, the chapter uses the results of ethnographic fieldwork conducted as part of a larger project on Twelver Shii Muslim transnational networks that operate between Britain and the Middle East.

## Religion and diaspora

Eickelman and Piscatori (1990), reflecting on the nature of travelling in Muslim societies, observe how certain forms of travel are enjoined by the Islamic tradition, such as the annual pilgrimage to Mecca (*hajj*), visitations of the shrines of Sufi saints or Shii Imams (*ziyara*) and journeying as part of one's religious training, in search for knowledge (*rihlat talab al-'ilm*). Given the religious significance travelling obtains under these circumstances, the journey is not merely an act of moving from one place to another, but it becomes 'an act of imagination' (Eickelman and Piscatori, 1990, p xii), loaded with meanings beyond its mere physical dislocation. Alluding to the labour migration into Europe of people from the traditional heartland of the Muslim world, they also mention the subsequent 'changes in religious institutions and practices' (Eickelman and Piscatori, 1990, p 5) that have occurred, and illustrate the impact the physical displacement has had on the religious imagination of Muslim migrants. Revealing ambivalent dynamics, 'travel creates boundaries and distinctions, even as travellers believe they are transcending them' (Eickelman and Piscatori, 1990, p 5). The travellers' crossing of boundaries leads to their encounter with 'others' and to a refined understanding of 'difference and similarity' (Eickelman and Piscatori, 1990, p 5).

These dynamics of 'crossing and dwelling' (Tweed, 2006) are further heightened when the journeying is not temporary but leads to a permanent dwelling, as diasporic communities emerge spatially distant from the homeland. The paradigmatic Jewish experience of diaspora illustrates how the involuntary dislocation of a people impinges on their religious imagination, as their exile or diaspora is enriched with soteriological meanings, interpreted as divine punishment for failure to uphold the law and as a redemptive path with return to the homeland as promise of final deliverance (Baumann, 2010, pp 20-2). The Jewish paradigm also exemplifies the central predicament of diasporic communities: how to maintain a sense of communal identity when dispersed, and how to adapt to the new environment without loosing one's communal identity (Vertovec, 2009, p 131). This 'diasporic duality of continuity and change' (Vertovec, 2010, p 64) contains two contradictory trajectories – on the one hand, diasporic displacement may result in a heightened awareness of one's difference and in an affirmation of one's distinct identity, further amplifying one's particular religious identity in the diaspora, for example. Being placed as a diasporic minority in an alien context may also yield discursive and pragmatic readjustments in response to the specific challenges the new environment poses that may also feed back to the religious discourses and practices in the homeland (Vertovec, 2009, p 141).

However, the dynamics of diasporic displacement and transformation cannot be reduced to simplistic polarities of preservation vs adaptation, homeland vs diaspora, centre vs periphery. The classical 'triadic relationship' of diasporic communities as a nexus of (1) members of a self-identified group in a particular local context, (2) their dispersed co-members across the world and (3) their homeland or original context from which they have come (Vertovec, 2009, p 133) does not sufficiently capture the de-territorialising and re-territorialising processes of 'crossing and dwelling' either. At the same time, diaspora is utilised politically by migrant communities and postmodern theoreticians (Bhabha, 2004, pp 199-244) to challenge mono-cultural and hegemonic discursive constructions of national identities, and to denote the hybridity, multiplicity and fluidity that mark identities in a globalising world. However, such an approach does not sufficiently account for the continuous salience of nation-states, their physical and ideational boundaries, the senses of belonging they still evoke and the strategies of exclusion and inclusion with which they operate.

Pnina Werbner's (2002, 2004, 2010) work takes account of the multilayered dimensions of diasporic formations. She develops the notion of 'complex diasporas' to articulate their '*social heterogeneity*' (2010, p 74; original emphasis), the convergence and co-existence of different, often mutually exclusive, discourses in diasporic communities, the dynamic and chaordical processes involved in their formation, and their '*dual orientation*' (2010, p 74; original emphasis): their efforts to represent their communities and to be recognised as such in the new diasporic context while at the same time maintaining transnational links and the community's diasporic identity; diasporas are involved in the developments of their countries of origin, reflecting, influencing and responding to them. While the transnational orientation and links of diasporas seems to undermine the boundaries and effectiveness of the nation-state, the latter is still an important frame of reference – both in terms of the original national homeland of diasporas and the socio-political and legal context in which diasporas are formed outside thereof. As such, diasporas are 'both ethnic-parochial *and* cosmopolitan' (Werbner 2010, p 75; original emphasis). The presence of diasporas also challenges the assumption of a single national public sphere. They prove the diversity of public arenas and various sub-cultures allowing for the communal and public articulation of subaltern groups and communities. In addition, the public arena is not just constituted of rational beings but also contains an emotional and affective side that is equally important, in particular in relation to the covalence of religion and politics.

Werbner's notion of complex diasporas illustrates that diasporic spaces are embedded in complex dynamics that are not sufficiently encapsulated in discursive dichotomies around diasporic formations. Scholarship often focuses on the patterns of continuity in diasporic communities in their efforts to recreate their homeland as opposed to changes resulting from generational dynamics. Often, typologies of diasporic communities are created differentiating between those that are progressive and those that are regressive, those that are successful agents of integration into the host societies and those that oppose integration. In a similar vein, a dichotomy is created between diasporic communities that identify themselves with a transnational religious community rather than attempting to create localised national religious identities post-migration; in the context of the Muslim presence in Britain, for example, this is articulated in the apparent tension between loyalty to the *umma*, the imagined global community of Muslims, as opposed to the development of a 'British Islam'. Another dichotomy juxtaposes hybridity and purity based on the notion that folk, popular or non-institutional forms of religiosity are experimental and diffuse while established religious institutions emphasise orthodoxy and doctrinal purity.

## From diaspora to multilocality

What alternative frameworks are available to overcome the potential conceptual limitations of the term diaspora? Metcalf (1996) chooses the notion of 'space' to engage in an analysis of the emergence of Muslim communities in Europe and North America that includes not only the discourses of Muslim elites, but also the daily practices of Muslim migrants. Space is thereby multidimensional, encompassing

> ... the "social space" of networks and identities created as individuals interact in new contexts, as well as the "cultural space" that emerges in a wide variety of ways as Muslims interact with one another and with the wider community. In some cases the interaction entails "physical space": the very right of residence, the erection of community buildings, the processions that mark an urban area. (Metcalf, 1996, pp 2-3)

While Metcalf's use of the notion of 'space' remains preliminary, it already points at the potential use of a spatial toolkit to study diasporic religions.

Most recently, Kim Knott (2005a, b, 2009) conceptualised the relation between space and religion in order to advance a spatial methodology in Religious Studies. Knott (2005b, p 3) makes the observation that diaspora and migration are themselves spatial terms describing the dispersal or movement of people from one place to another in order to propose a spatial methodology for the study of the history and politics of diaspora and migration. The particular challenge of studying diasporic communities in a globalised world of 'time-space compression' or 'distanciation' (Vásquez, 2010, p 280) lies in their very multilocality: they exist in a particular locality but are not restricted to a location because of their transnational connections. Based on reconceptualisations of space and place by Michel Foucault (1994) and Henri Lefebvre (1974) and their reception within Human Geography (Tuan, 1977; Massey, 2005) and Religious Studies (Smith, 1978), Knott, together with Thomas Tweed (1997, 2006) and Manuel

Vásquez (2010), conceives a spatial methodology as an analytical framework to study diasporic religious communities. Place is thereby neither conceived as mere local context or 'passive container' (Knott, 2005a, p 7) that hosts particular religious communities nor regarded as static locality demarcated by fixed boundaries of nation or community. To overcome the impression of a static and localised approach to the study of religious communities in a particular place, Knott prefers an understanding of space that is dynamic and multidimensional, containing – following Lefebvre – physical, social and discursive dimensions (Knott, 2005a, pp 35-58). Knott's (2005a, pp 46-50) primary interest is in the spatial strategies religious communities adopt to enter the secular space of European societies, and in the spaces that religious communities create themselves in particular locations and the dynamics processes involved therein.

Vásquez' and Tweed's foci lie in the global–local nexus and in the transnational connections of diasporic religious communities. Based on his study of a Marian shrine built by Catholic Cubans in Miami, Tweed (1997) distinguishes between three levels in which diasporic religions operate:

- *Locative:* the actual shrine that Catholic Cubans built in Miami to maintain their Catholic-Cuban identity in the diasporic context of primarily Protestant America.
- *Trans-locative:* the shrine faces Cuba and its murals depict the history of the country, thereby symbolising the horizontal connection of the diaspora to a real and imagined homeland.
- *Supra-locative:* as the shrine is discursively construed as a space to connect vertically with God, it acts as a spatial representation of the soteriological and redemptive meanings the Cubans assign to their enforced exile. Nostalgic of pre-Communist Cuba, they conceive their exile as part of a wider cosmic struggle between good and evil.

Tweed's distinction between the locative, trans-locative and supra-locative levels of diasporic religions mirrors Knott's conception of space as containing physical, social and discursive dimensions. Despite its benefits, Tweed's dimensions do not sufficiently pay attention to the power relations inherent to the formation of diasporic communities (Vásquez, 2009). Vásquez (2008, 2010) suggests an approach that introduces the notion of networks to illustrate both the locative, trans-locative and supra-locative dimensions of transnational diasporic communities and the importance and persistence of power relations in their de-territorialising and re-territorialising dynamics. Vásquez defines networks as 'social fields' (2010, p 299) to which individual actors have different access and entertain a diverse range of relations. Networks can be characterised by a high degree of institutionalisation with clear hierarchies and membership criteria or be highly amorphous with permeable boundaries and decentralised patterns of authority. Despite their structural differences, networks delimitate trajectories of actions and discourses and serve as spaces that provide meaning to their members through shared practices, discourses, symbols, rituals etc. Their power relations manifest in conflicting claims to authority and status within these networks and in competition with other networks. They can also serve as alternative social spheres outside of state and society, challenging 'dominant secular readings of civil society and citizenship' (Vásquez, 2010, p 302).

Tweed's distinction between the different spatial orientations of diasporic religious communities has the advantage of taking both the local context in which these communities are embedded seriously while at the same time illustrating how transnational connections and orientations are articulated. At the same time, Tweed emphasises the 'religious' dimension of diasporic religions with the notion of the supra-locative. The Cuban community around the Marian shrine in Miami is not just a political group or a cultural club but a religious community that reads its experience of exile, the political tribulations of Cuba and the need to maintain one's identity in the diaspora in religious terms using the imagery, rituals and language of Latin American Catholicism. However, the locative also contains complex layers that Tweed does not sufficiently disentangle. Diasporic communities are situated in an immediate local context, such as a particular neighbourhood, establish links with other social actors in an urban area and can be engaged in very localised forms of religious, social or political activism. At the same time, they are also placed in the wider context of the nation-state with its own political and legal culture, particular church–state relations and various types of government interaction with religious organisations and institutions. Hence, the locative is both local and national. Tweed's approach also contains the tendency – apart from not sufficiently paying attention to power relations inherent in these networks – to ignore dynamics of 'lived religion' on the ground, best accessed through ethnographic research. Including the study of 'lived religion' as constituent in the research on diasporic religions moves the focus away from normative discourses of often-male elites in organised structures of religion.

In writing about the place of religion in British Asian diasporas, Seán McLoughlin and John Zavos (2014) suggest a discursive shift from diaspora to multilocality. In order to give sufficient justice to the various levels of locality and to include religious practices and discourses outside of organised religion, both propose a multilocal configuration of diasporic communities that unfold on four spatial scales:

- On the very *local level*, immigration has led to the formation of ethnically, culturally and religiously diverse neighbourhood communities in urban areas. Therefore, the physicality of urban landscapes has changed as a result of demographic transformations, leading to 'the formation of neighbourhood congregations and "communities" in the context of urban resettlement' (McLoughlin and Zavos, 2014, p 160).
- On both the *local and the national level*, religious communities interact with state and society, particularly in terms of the politics of recognition and participation in the context of British multiculturalism. Diaspora religious communities seek to be recognised by the state and other stakeholders in society as representing 'their' community.
- On a *global level*, religious organisations are characterised by trans- and multilocal networking and activism with their countries of origin or other diaspora communities across the world.

- On a *personal level*, diaspora communities contain 'demotic' (literally, 'of the people') processes and discourses (Baumann, 1996) of individual and collective religiosities, 'the informal and negotiated utterances and performativity of individuals and non-institutionalized collectives' (McLoughlin and Zavos, 2014, p 161) that challenge normative discourses and practices promulgated within organised communities.

## The Shia mile of London

The usefulness of these recent theoretical reflections on the development of a spatial methodology is discussed in relation to research on transnational Twelver Shii Muslim[1] networks that operate between Britain and the Middle East. The local starting point is the so-called Shia mile of London in the borough of Brent, in the northwest of the city. In the last 30 years Brent has become not just the European but also one of the global hubs of transnational Twelver Shii Islam. There are at least 20 Shii community centres located in Brent representing different national backgrounds but also different religious and political factions within contemporary Shii Islam. The vast majority of these centres are run and frequented by Iraqi Shiis who began to arrive in Brent in the 1970s and have continued to settle in the area as a result of their oppression in the regime of Saddam Hussein and also due to the most recent sectarian violence post-2003. With Iraqis being dominant, other ethnic and national groups likewise frequent and run various community centres, including Gulf Arab, Iranian, Afghan and South Asian Shiis. Following Vásquez, these community centres are part of wider religious networks and constitute social fields that act locally, nationally and transnationally while also containing supra-locative dimensions; they are the diasporic headquarters of Shii Islamist parties, offices representing senior Shii clerical authorities based in the Middle East, charitable and educational foundations, institutions representing the Islamic Republic of Iran and grassroots and youth networks.

To investigate the physical, social and discursive dimensions of spaces inhabited by these networks, Tweed's distinction between the locative, trans-locative and supra-locative levels of diasporic religions is employed here as a further illustration of the different spatial scales in which these networks operate. Building on Tweed's scheme, however, this chapter also includes Knott and Vásquez' emphasis on power relations within these networks as central to the analysis. In addition, demotic processes to promote 'alternative' understandings of Shii religiosity to 'resist their marginalization and disciplining by secular nation-states, neo-orthodox movements and consumer capitalism' (McLoughlin and Zavos, 2014, p 172) can also be observed and need to be taken into consideration.

## *The locative: Both local and national*

The starting point is the spatial manifestations of these networks in Brent in the form of congregational centres and offices, educational initiatives for both members of the network, other Shiis and the wider public, outreach activities such as participation in interfaith dialogue, and other various mediation activities from print publications, TV stations and internet presences. In the institutional field of Shii Islam in Britain the Al-Khoei Foundation, based in Brent and established in 1989, has been the major Shii actor in the politics of multicultural recognition, being the quasi-official representative of Twelver Shii Muslims in the UK. As the centre of a global network of different institutions, the Al-Khoei Foundation in London operates locally, nationally and internationally in its various outreach activities. Internationally, it is well connected to international organisations such as the United Nations (UN) Human Rights Council in Geneva, making regular interventions in its sessions, the Jordanian Royal Institute for Inter-Faith Studies, established by Hassan bin Talal, and Ali Al-Hashimi, the judicial and religious adviser to the President of the United Arab Emirates. These two latter relations have resulted in the Al-Khoei Foundation being involved in high-profile international inter-faith and Sunni–Shia intra-faith dialogue events.

Nationally, the Al-Khoei Foundation is usually approached by the British government and its various departments for advice on issues affecting Shii Muslims in Britain, and is also one of the founding members and only Shii organisation of the Mosques and Imams National Advisory Board (MINAB), an organisation founded after the London 7/7 bombings in 2005 in order to provide advice to mosque communities on how to meet professional standards in providing religious, pastoral and educational services to their congregations. The Foundation played a central role in the revision of the GCSE curriculum in Islam undertaken in 2015, ensuring that both Sunni and Shii Islam have an equal footing in the new Religious Education (RE) curriculum (Ofqual, 2015, pp 17-19).

On a local level, the Al-Khoei Foundation is involved in various inter-faith initiatives such as the London Inter Faith Centre, the Three Faiths Forum, the Faiths Forum for London or the Brent Inter Faith Network and other civic society actors such as the North London branch of Citizens UK. In October 2016, under the umbrella of the Faiths Forum for London, the Al-Khoei Foundation hosted the Jewish Sukkot festival in partnership with the neighbouring Brondesbury United Synagogue, with volunteers from both communities building a wooden booth on the premises of the Al-Khoei Foundation. The event was presented in the media as 'a historic first in the UK' (Cohen, 2016), an 'unprecedented partnership between a British mosque and synagogue' (Anonymous, 2016), as 'a London mosque has played host for a local synagogue's succah' (Cohen, 2016). This highly symbolic gesture to articulate the commitment of the Al-Khoei Foundation to break down barriers between Jews and Muslims in the UK was partially inspired by the rise of anti-Semitic and Islamophobic hate crimes following the Brexit referendum in June 2016. It was also meant to further buttress the moderate credentials of the Al-Khoei Foundation in a multicultural context in which 'faith is projected as "bridging" capital – a common denominator of the universal signifiers of respect for difference and spirituality' (McLoughlin and Zavos, 2014, p 175).

## *The trans-locative: 'Long-distance nationalism'*

The Shii Muslim networks in Brent are characterised by a high degree of transnational connectiveness and activism. They serve as conduits, proxies or representations of transnational networks and maintain a wide range of transnational links. A prime example of an institution engaged in 'long-distance nationalism' (Anderson, 1992) in Brent is Dar al-Islam, a Shii congregation and community centre that acts as the London base of the Islamic Dawa Party, the main Shii Islamist party in Iraq that has led the government since 2005. Being the official base of the Dawa Party, it was the main site of diasporic politics of Iraqi Shii Islamists in exile, and retains an important role as conduit between the Iraqi governing party and the Iraqi diaspora in London. Many members and attendees of Dar al-Islam have returned to Iraq and assumed important political, economic or cultural roles. The Prime Minister of Iraq, Haider al-Abadi lived for many decades in Brent and was affiliated to the centre, its former resident scholar and imam returned to Iraq to establish a private university, and other members now hold positions in government departments in Iraq. From the set-up of the community centre it is not really visible that this congregation is affiliated to the Dawa Party; it does not exhibit any Iraqi flags or other symbols of Iraqi national identity nor any images, slogans or logos of the party as such. One can only observe indirect signs suggesting a connection to the main Iraqi Shii Islamist party. On the office walls of the director of the congregation are photographs of important clerical authorities in the history of the party: Muhammad Baqir al-Sadr (1935-80), founder of the party that was established in Iraq in 1958, and Lebanese cleric Mohammad Hussein Fadlallah (1935-2010), the religious reference point for many of its members (Abd al-Jabbar, 2003). References to these two prominent clerical figures articulate the historical formation of the party and also serve as sources of religious legitimacy. This is particularly important to Islamists of the Dawa Party who are often suspected of entertaining a certain distance to clerical authorities in Shii Islam.

For McLoughlin and Zavos (2014, p 175), the transnational networking of diasporic communities can entail and articulate various modes of 'religious resistance to globalized modernity.' While the Dawa Party has been in the Iraqi government and has been made responsible for the rise of sectarian politics in Iraq, as an Islamist party it shares similar ideological roots with Sunni Islamist movements, and retains the pan-Islamic appeal of political Islam to a certain extent. This also becomes manifest in the more political activities held at Dar al-Islam. In June 2015, for example, the centre hosted a conference organised by the Islamic Unity Forum, a London-based organisation bringing Shii and Sunni Islamist activists together. The conference included Sunni and Shii religious scholars as well as activists from both denominations. The proceedings of the conference articulated support for pan-Islamism against Western neocolonial policies in the Middle East, evidenced in the Sykes–Picot Agreement of 1916, the creation of Israel and the Saudi-led war against Yemen. While Dar al-Islam exhibits a strong sense of 'long-distance nationalism', it oscillates in its activities between the promotion of sectarian discourses and politics within an Iraqi context and a sense of pan-Islamic anti-imperialist resistance to Western political hegemony over the Middle East.

## *The supra-locative: The production of competing Shia religious imaginaires*

Apart from the emplacement of these networks in the urban area of Brent and their various transnational connections, they also operate on a supra-locative level. For Tweed, the supra-locative constitutes the specifically 'religious' vertical relationship of a diasporic religious community with God and the discursive permeation of their diasporic experience with soteriological connotations. In the context of this chapter, the supra-locative is understood as a reference to discursive and ideational conceptions of 'home' as a space that transcends both the locative and the trans-locative. In this context, home entails both 'a realm of concrete locality and everyday experience' and 'a more ideational, symbolic or discursive realm' (Stock, 2010, p 26). Bringing more conceptual clarity to core ideas in the study of transnationalism and diaspora, Vertovec (2009) defines transnationalism as referring to the networks and interactions occurring between the homeland and the diaspora – identified here with the trans-locative. Diaspora, however, is understood as 'an imagined connection' (Vertovec, 2009, p 136) with the place of origin or a wider community that can be real but is also imagined in the sense that it purports strong emotive connotations and is based on collective memory. Jonathan Z. Smith characterises diasporic religion 'as utopian in the strictest sense of the word, a religion of "nowhere", of transcendence' (quoted in Vásquez 2010, p 272). While even diasporic religion is not entirely placeless, as previous discussions have shown, but always emplaced at various locations, Smith highlights an element of diasporic religion that transcends both locality and multilocality.

As an example, McLoughlin characterises the increasing tendency among British Pakistani Muslims to identify with the *umma* as their imagined mythical and historical homeland as an expression of Brah's 'homing desire' (Brah, 1996, pp 179-80; McLouglin, 2010, p 225). The *umma* becomes the locus of a trans-locative and supra-locative religious imaginaire, the spatial manifestation of a de-territorialised and universalised form of Islam. This Islam is utopian in the sense that it transcends historical, cultural, ethnic and geographical boundaries, yearns for a revival of a unified *umma* and turns the historical role model into a template for global Muslim politics (Mandaville, 2007). However, the Shii historical experience of marginalisation and status as a minority view within Islam – thoroughly internalised in the Shii collective memory – creates different dynamics in contradistinction to global (Sunni-)Muslim politics. Karbala in Southern Iraq – the place where Husayn, the third Shii Imam and grandson of Muhammad was murdered in 680CE – rather than Mecca serves as 'mythico-historical and territorial orientation' (McLoughlin, 2010, p 223) for Shii Muslims.

Rituals play a key role in the creation of competing Shii religious imaginaires that constitute the supra-locative dimension of these transnational networks. Certain congregations make efforts to demarcate themselves from both the clerical establishment and various expressions of political Islam in Shiism, whether in Iraq or Iran. The so-called Shiraziyyin constitute a global network of clerical families, their followers and political groups who adhere to the religious and socio-political teachings of Muhammad al-Shirazi (1928-2001) and his younger brothers. Initially with close ideological ties to the leader of the Islamic Revolution Ayatollah Khomeini (1902-89), Shirazi grew increasingly disillusioned by the Iranian regime and articulated his opposition to Khomeini, in particular the war against Iraq. He was placed under house arrest in Iran and died in 2001. His younger brother Sadiq al-Shirazi has acted as clerical leader of the Shiraziyyin since then. In Brent the Hussainiat al-Rasool al-Adham had been the community centre congregating Shiraziyyin based in London.

Members of the congregation are proud of the special atmosphere of the centre that also attracts Shiis of different backgrounds who would usually attend other congregations. While in other community centres efforts are made to control and subdue the passionate display of emotions during ritual performances, those leading and involved in their performance in Rasool al-Adham encourage the congregations to express their religious fervour in their strongest possible terms. In addition, ritual practices are performed in Rasool al-Adham that are either frowned upon or outwardly rejected by mainstream clerical authorities and political actors in the Middle East and their representations in Brent. The controversial practices include self-flagellation, by hitting the forehead with a sword to cause bleeding, and walking on hot coals. In this sense, the particular 'aesthetic style' (Meyer, 2009, p 9) of Rasool al-Adham positions the Shiraziyyin uniquely within the Shii field in Brent.

This ritually performed 'aesthetic style' also delivers a political message. The Shiraziyyin and their clerical leaders have entertained difficult relations with the Islamic Republic of Iran following the estrangement of Muhammad al-Shirazi from Khomeini and more so when Sayyid Ali Khamenei became Supreme Leader of Iran in 1989. Khamenei is one of the few senior clerics in contemporary Shii Islam who has explicitly declared the performance of self-flagellation unlawful (*haram*). As a consequence congregations affiliated to Iran or close to it have shunned this practice. Maintaining its performance by the Shiraziyyin is therefore also an act of political defiance, rejecting the hegemonic ambitions of the political establishment in Iran to exercise transnational control over Shii Islam. The Shiraziyyin also reject initiatives by the Islamic Republic and its clerical representatives to tone down the emotional intensity of Shii rituals and their sectarian tone to avoid antagonising and alienating Sunni Muslims.

The Shiraziyyin in London employ Shia ritual practices as 'demotic, embodied practices' (McLoughlin and Zavos, 2014, p 173) to distinguish themselves from other factions in Shii Islam and to claim their unique niche within the Shii field of Brent locally and globally within the wider Shii Muslim world. The performance of these rituals is also seen as a marker of 'cultural authenticity' (Rizvi, 2010, p 1306) against the adulteration of Shii Islam by representatives of political Shiism, whether the Dawa Party in Iraq or the Islamic Republic of Iran. The demotic Shii space of the Shiraziyyin in Rasool al-Adham in London creates at the same time 'the idea of an alternative, utopian, as well as potentially millenarian and apocalyptic, moral space exceeding the limits of their diasporic location and minority status' (McLoughlan and Zavos, 2014, pp 170-1).

## Conclusion

Within Religious Studies there has been a long tradition of discussing the relationship between space and religion (Knott, 2005a, pp 95-104; Vásquez, 2010, pp 261-73), articulated in particular in the influential distinction between sacred and profane space (Durkheim, 2001 [1912]; Eliade 1959). This chapter has discussed recent contributions to revise these conceptualisations around space and religion in order to develop a robust theoretical framework to understand the nature and modus operandi of multilocal religious communities, organisations and networks, and the various spatial scales in which their activities and discourses unfold. Combining contributions by Knott, Tweed, Vásquez and McLoughlin and Zavos, this chapter has attempted to make these debates fruitful for the study of transnational Twelver Shii Muslim networks that are located in Brent, northwest London, but are transnationally connected. These contributions are equally useful in the study of other diasporic religions as evidenced in the works of the authors discussed above who have researched Latin American church communities in North America or British South Asian diasporic communities, whether Hindu, Sikh or Muslim.

Combining these contributions is meant to further new spatial approaches in understanding diasporic and transnational religions that take their various spatial dimensions seriously: their local manifestations in a particular neighbourhood, their engagement with national politics, their transnational connectivities and their production of supra-locative religious imaginaires that transcend the local, national and transnational. Such a spatial approach takes power relations seriously – around these networks, in terms of the state governance of minority religions and ways to assign them to the periphery, and within these networks in which particular groups are placed or position themselves outside centres of authority.

## Acknowledgements

The Gerda Henkel Foundation funded this project. Fieldwork in London was conducted between September 2014 and October 2016.

## Note

[1] Islam consists of two major denominations, Sunnis and Shiis. Shiis are further divided into various sub-groups such as Ismailis, Zaydis and Twelver Shiis. Twelver Shiis are distinguished from Sunnis (and other Shiis) by their beliefs in a line of twelve successive leaders of the Muslim community following the death of the Prophet Muhammad. These twelve imams (from the Arabic *imam*, 'leader') were male descendants of the Prophet and appointed by their predecessors. For an overview, see Haider (2014, pp 51-100).

## References

Abd al-Jabbar, F.A. (2003) *The Shi'ite movement in Iraq*, London: Saqi Books.

Anderson, B. (1992) *Long-distance nationalism: World capitalism and the rise of identity politics*, Amsterdam: Centre for Asian Studies Amsterdam.

Anonymous (2016) 'Constructing cohesion: Sukkah built at mosque as communities come together', *Asian Express Newspaper*, 24 October (www.asianexpress.co.uk/2016/10/constructing-cohesion-sukkah-built-at-mosque-as-communities-come-together/).

Baumann, G. (1996) *Contesting culture: Discourses of identity in multi-ethnic London*, Cambridge: Cambridge University Press.

Baumann, M. (2010) 'Exile', in K. Knott and S. McLoughlin (eds) *Diasporas: Concepts, intersections, identities*, London and New York: Zed Books, pp 19-23.

Bhabha, H. (2004) *The location of culture*, London and New York: Routledge.

Brah, A. (1996) *Cartographies of diaspora: Contesting identities*, London and New York: Routledge.

Cohen, J. (2016) 'London mosque hosts Jewish community for Succot', *Jewish News Online*, 24 October (http://jewishnews.timesofisrael.com/london-mosque-hosts-jewish-community-for-succot/).

Durkheim, E. (2001 [1912]) *The elementary forms of religious life*, Oxford: Oxford University Press.

Eickelman, D.F. and Piscatori, J. (eds) (1990) *Muslim travellers: Pilgrimage, migration, and the religious imagination*, Berkeley and Los Angeles, CA: University of California Press.

Eliade, M. (1959) *The sacred and the profane: The nature of religion*, Orlando, FL: Harcourt.

Foucault, M. (1994) 'Des espaces autres', in *Dits et écrits: 1954-1988*, vol 4 (1980-88), Paris: Éditions Gallimard, pp 752-62.

Haider, N. (2014) *Shi'i Islam: An introduction*, Cambridge: Cambridge University Press.

Knott, K. (2005a) *The location of religion: A spatial analysis*, London and New York: Routledge.

Knott, K. (2005b) 'Towards a history and politics of diasporas and migration: A grounded spatial approach', Paper presented at 'Flows and Spaces', Annual Conference of the Royal Geographical Society/Institute of British Geographers, London, 30 August-2 September.

Knott, K. (2009) 'From locality to location and back again: A spatial journey in the study of religion', *Religion*, vol 39, no 2, pp 154-60.

Lefebvre, H. (1974) *La production de l'espace*, Paris: Anthropos.

Mandaville, P. (2007) *Global political Islam*, London and New York: Routledge.

Massey, D. (2005) *For space*, London: Sage.

Meyer, B. (ed.) (2009) *Aesthetic formations: Media, religion, and the senses*, New York: Palgrave Macmillan.

McLoughlin, S. (2010) 'Muslim travellers: Homing desire, the *umma* and British Pakistanis', in K. Knott and S. McLoughlin (eds) *Diasporas: Concepts, intersections, identities*, London and New York: Zed Books, pp 223-9.

McLoughlin, S. and Zavos, J. (2014) 'Writing religion in British Asian diasporas', in S. McLoughlin, W. Gould, A.J. Kabir and E. Tomalin (eds) *Writing the city in British Asian diasporas*, London and New York: Routledge, pp 158-78.

Metcalf, B.D. (ed) (1996), *Making Muslim space in North America and Europe*, Berkeley and Los Angeles, CA: University of California Press.

Ofqual (Office of Qualifications and Examinations Regulations) (2015) *GCSE subject level conditions and requirements for Religious Studies*, Coventry: Ofqual.

Rizvi, S. (2010) 'Political mobilization and the Shi'i religious establishment (*marja'iyya*)', *International Affairs*, vol 86, no 6, pp 1299-313.

Smith. J.Z. (1978) *Map is not territory: Studies in the history of religions*, Chicago, IL: University of Chicago Press.

Stock, F. (2010) 'Home and memory', in K. Knott and S. McLoughlin (eds) *Diasporas: Concepts, intersections, identities*, London and New York: Zed Books, pp 24-8.

Tuan, Y-F. (1977) *Space and place: The perspective of experience*, Minneapolis, MN: University of Minnesota Press.

Tweed, T.A. (1997) *Our lady of exile: Diasporic religion at a Cuban Catholic shrine in Miami*, Oxford and New York: Oxford University Press.

Tweed, T.A. (2006) *Crossing and dwelling: A theory of religion*, Cambridge, MA: Harvard University Press.

Vásquez, M.A. (2008) 'Studying religion in motion: A networks approach', *Method & Theory in the Study of Religion*, vol 20, no 2, pp 151-84.

Vásquez, M.A. (2009) 'The limits of the hydrodynamics of religion', *Journal of the American Academy of Religion*, vol 77, no 2, pp 434-45.

Vásquez, M.A. (2010) *More than belief: A materialist theory of religion*, Oxford and New York: Oxford University Press.

Vertovec, S. (2009) *Transnationalism*, London and New York: Routledge.

Vertovec, S. (2010) 'Cosmopolitanism', in K. Knott and S. McLoughlin (eds) *Diasporas: Concepts, intersections, identities*, London and New York: Zed Books, pp 63-8.

Werbner, P. (2002) 'The place which is diaspora: Citizenship, religion and gender in the making of chaordic transnationalism', *Journal of Ethnic and Migration Studies*, vol 28, no 1, pp 119-33.

Werbner, P. (2004) 'Theorising complex diasporas: Purity and hybridity in the South Asian public sphere in Britain', *Journal of Ethnic and Migration Studies*, vol 30, no 5, pp 895-911.

Werbner, P. (2010) 'Complex diasporas', in K. Knott and S. McLoughlin (eds) *Diasporas: Concepts, intersections, identities*, London and New York: Zed Books, pp 74-8.

# PART 2: RE-IMAGINING PUBLIC POLICY AND PRACTICE

# FIVE

# Law and religion: A survey of cases in the UK and what they reveal

Lucy Vickers

## Introduction

Religion and belief enjoys protection in international and domestic law as part of a framework of fundamental human rights, with freedom of religion and belief found within all major human rights treaties. To this has been added a legal guarantee of equality on grounds of religion and belief. To an extent, freedom of religion and belief, and equality on the grounds of religion can be understood to be complementary rights, founded on the notions of dignity, autonomy and equality. Nonetheless, these different foundations for protecting religion or belief can also be in tension with each other: for example, religions do not always recognise the fundamental rights and freedoms of others, such as rights not to be discriminated against on grounds of status, gender, sexual orientation or other grounds. Equally, tension arises when religious-ethos employers are prevented from using faith as a factor in recruitment, leading to restrictions on religious freedom. As a result, determining the boundaries for proper legal treatment of freedom of religion and belief, equality on grounds of religion and belief and equality on other grounds can be complex.

In this chapter I consider how these different rights have been treated in three areas in which cases have arisen in the UK: the wearing of religious dress to work; conscientious objection to particular work tasks on the basis of religion; and the refusal of services on grounds of sexual orientation for reasons related to religion. I then identify some of the broader social and policy themes that have come before the courts, and suggest a framework that may help courts to resolve some of the complexities with which they are faced.

## The legal framework

Traditionally, human rights have been understood to form part of the protection for citizens from the power of the state, and it has been within this context that religious freedom rights have materialised. Article 9 of the European Convention on Human Rights (ECHR) protects the right to freedom of thought, conscience and religion, and recognises that this includes the right to manifest religion or belief 'either alone or in community with others', so that the right applies to religious groups as well as individuals. The right has tended to be engaged with regard to manifestations of belief – in particular, the wearing of religious symbols and conscientious objection to certain work tasks.

More recently, religion and belief have been protected as part of a framework of equality rights, enforceable between non-state actors such as service providers and service users, and employers and employees. This protection is provided in the UK by the Equality Act 2010 that protects against direct and indirect discrimination, harassment and victimisation on grounds of religion or belief.

Direct discrimination occurs where a person is treated less favourably on grounds of religion and belief, for example, where employers or service providers refuse to employ religious staff or refuse services to religious individuals. Indirect discrimination occurs where a provision, requirement or practice puts people of a particular religion or belief at a particular disadvantage compared with others. It can be justified where there is a legitimate aim for the requirement and the means of achieving the aim are appropriate and necessary (Equality Act 2010, Section 19). Examples include where the employer imposes requirements in terms of uniforms or hours of work with which it is difficult for those of particular religions to comply. Any such requirements must be justified as a proportionate means to meet a legitimate aim.

## Religious dress codes at work

In the employment context, one of the most common issues involving religion or belief relates to dress codes (van Ooijen, 2102). For example, some workplaces impose restrictions on the wearing of religious symbols such as headscarves or turbans, to accord with a workplace uniform; alternatively, dress codes may require female staff to wear skirts or otherwise breach religious dress codes. Legally such rules are treated as potentially indirectly discriminatory and need to be justified as a proportionate means of achieving a legitimate aim. In determining its proportionality, the court needs to consider whether a restriction on dress interferes with Article 9 ECHR rights given that under Section 6 of the Human Rights Act 1998 legislation should be interpreted to comply with the ECHR.

The case of *Azmi v Kirklees Metropolitan Borough Council* illustrates how a restriction on religious clothing can be justified as a proportionate means to achieve a legitimate aim. Azmi, a teaching assistant, was dismissed for refusing to remove her *niqab* when assisting in class. She was unsuccessful in her claims of direct and indirect discrimination. The court accepted that the restriction on face coverings put Azmi at a particular disadvantage when compared with others, but held that the *prima facie* indirect discrimination was justified. The restriction was proportionate given the need to uphold the interests of the children in having the best possible education, and for this they needed to have good non-verbal communication by being able to see her face. In effect, the court undertook a balancing exercise between the interest in the religious freedom of the teaching assistant and the interests of the school children in clear non-verbal communication from staff.

A similar approach, based on balancing competing interests, can be seen in *Eweida et al v the United Kingdom*, which involved four different cases brought from the UK to the European Court of Human Rights (ECtHR). Two of the cases involved dress codes. Eweida, a member of the check-in staff for British Airways, was refused permission to wear a cross over her uniform. Although Eweida was unsuccessful before the UK courts, the ECtHR held that the restriction was not proportionate: factors that aided this decision included the fact that other forms of religious dress such as headscarves and turbans were allowed, and the argument that the employer needed to maintain its corporate image was not very strong when weighed against Eweida's freedom of religion. In comparison, in the second dress code case, Chaplin, a nurse, was required to remove the cross that she wore on a chain around her neck for health and safety reasons, and the Court held these reasons were sufficient to outweigh the employee's religious interests.

The wearing of religious symbols is a common way for religion and belief to be manifested in the wider environment, and evidence suggests that the law in this regard is reasonably well understood and religious symbols widely accommodated in the UK, including in the judiciary and police (Mitchell et al, 2015). The UK cases suggest that a fairly practical balance has been struck between the interests of staff who wish to manifest religion at work, and the business needs of the employer. Where there is no good reason to the contrary, staff may wear religious symbols, but where employers can provide good reasons, such as health and safety requirements or the requirements of effective service delivery, restrictions on religious symbols at work are likely to be proportionate. In contrast, elsewhere in Europe restrictions on religious dress at work are widely imposed, particularly in the public sector (van Ooijen, 2012).

## *Conscientious objection*

A second area in which law and religion questions have arisen is that of conscientious objection to work tasks, where staff have sought, for religious reasons, to be excused from performing aspects of their jobs. Sometimes these requests are relatively simple such as requests to be excused from selling alcohol or handling meat products. These are treated legally in the same way as requests relating to uniforms: where proportionate, employers may refuse such requests, but a refusal when it would be easy to accommodate may be indirectly discriminatory. In assessing the proportionality of any refusal to allow a change in duties, a court can consider all the facts of the case, such as the ease with which others can be found to cover for the task without disadvantage or disruption to others, whether the individual can be redeployed to other duties and how central the task is to the job in question. For example, it would be unlikely to be justified to refuse to exempt a university lecturer from serving alcohol at a reception for new students: the request does not relate to a core aspect of the job, and it will be relatively easy to find someone else to serve the refreshments. In contrast, it would be proportionate to refuse to accommodate a publican who refuses to serve alcohol.

More complex cases have involved the refusal of a task on grounds that themselves are discriminatory. For example, cases have arisen in several jurisdictions involving marriage registrars who wish to be exempted from carrying out civil partnerships due to religious objections to same-sex relationships. These cases, too, are treated legally as cases of indirect discrimination; the neutral requirement to carry out civil partnerships causes disadvantage to the particular religious employee because he or she cannot, for religious reasons, comply. Although potentially more problematic, as they raise issues of balancing between two competing equality rights, the UK courts have found there to be no obligation on the employer to accommodate a request for such an exemption on the part of the employee. The restriction on opting out of work tasks on religious grounds has been found to be proportionate as a means to achieve the legitimate aim of equal treatment on grounds of sexual orientation.

The case of *Ladele v Islington Borough Council*, heard with *Eweida* before the ECtHR, illustrates the approach of the courts. Ladele was refused permission to be excused from carrying out civil partnerships on the basis of her religious beliefs. The Court held that the refusal to accommodate Ladele's request was justified as the employer was entitled to rely on its policy of requiring all staff to offer services to all service users regardless of sexual orientation. This decision has been contentious, in part because Ms Ladele was already in employment when the requirement to perform civil partnerships was introduced, and accommodation of her type of request was allowed in other local authorities. However, in terms of the legal approach, the approach is similar to other indirect discrimination cases; the requirement that Ladele perform civil partnerships was potentially indirectly discriminatory, but it was justified as a proportionate means to protect the equality rights of others. Although it is perfectly possible to imagine a different outcome from that balancing exercise, the legal approach is based on the balancing of competing interests to achieve a proportionate result, and has the potential to be sensitive to the individual facts of the case.

## Refusal of services

A third area in which courts have been involved in regulating the relationship between law and religion relates to provision of services by businesses run on religions lines. Services have at times been refused because of the customer's sexual orientation. The first case involved the refusal by Christians who ran a Bed & Breakfast to allow same-sex couples to share double-bedded rooms (*Bull & Anor v Hall & Anor*). The UK Supreme Court ruled that this amounted to direct discrimination on grounds of sexual orientation, which is unlawful under the Equality Act 2010. The Bed & Breakfast owners would only let double-bedded rooms to married couples, because to do otherwise would conflict with their religious beliefs regarding sexual conduct. They also argued that if they were found to have acted unlawfully, this would undermine their right to manifest their religious beliefs under Article 9 of the ECHR. The Supreme Court found that the restrictions on letting double rooms to same-sex couples amounted to direct discrimination on grounds of sexual orientation, and was therefore unlawful.

A second case involving the refusal of services to members of the public because of sexual orientation concerned a bakery (Ashers) that refused to bake a cake because the cake was to bear the slogan 'Support Gay Marriage'. The Court of Appeal in Northern Ireland (CANI) held that Ashers had discriminated on grounds of sexual orientation in refusing to bake the cake because the refusal was for reasons of association with homosexuality (*Lee v McArthur & Ors*). The Court held that even though both homosexual and heterosexual people can support gay marriage, such support is indissociable from sexual orientation, and so discrimination on this ground is also unlawful. The case is complicated by the fact that it involves freedom of expression on the part of the bakery. However, the Court found that its decision was not incompatible with any such freedom of expression rights: the bakery was not required to promote or support gay marriage merely by providing a cake bearing the slogan. Moreover, even if a *prima facie* interference with free expression were to be found, this could be justified on the basis of the non-discrimination rights of the customer.

The case did involve a degree of conflict between the rights to religious freedom on the part of the bakery and its staff and the rights of the customer. However, the Court found that the bakery had discriminated against the customer, and that the baker's freedom of religion was adequately protected, particularly given that the services provided by the bakery were of a commercial nature.

## What do the cases reveal about the current relationship between law and religion?

These cases show that the law continues to struggle with some underlying issues that underpin the treatment of religion or belief in law. Particular issues that have arisen include how courts should deal with matters of religious doctrine, and how to deal with potential clashes between different rights. Underpinning these issues are broader questions relating to how best to understand religious claims, as equality or as human rights claims; whether there is a hierarchy developing between equality grounds; whether to treat the workplace as public or private in nature when it comes to religion claims; and whether it is either beneficial or indeed possible to create consistency in the treatment of religion or belief in law.

## Religious doctrine and 'core belief'

One matter that arises when law responds to religious claims is the question of the courts' role in deciding matters of religious doctrine. For example, in *Eweida* the domestic Court of Appeal had to consider a claim regarding the wearing of a cross, and the question arose as to whether this was a Christian requirement. The approach of the courts to questions of religious doctrine has varied. The traditional approach of human rights case law was to only protect practices that were required by the religion (*Arrowsmith v UK*). This had the potential to involve significant encroachment by courts into matters of religious doctrine. It could also give rise to additional problems for newer minority religions, where there may not be commonly accepted religious doctrines, making it difficult to prove whether a particular practice is required (Cumper, 2001).

However the court has more recently taken a more practical turn (Hill and Whistler, 2013), considering instead religious practice as understood by the applicant. This involves taking greater account of the subjective beliefs of the applicant as determinative of whether the practice amounted to a manifestation of religion (Sandberg, 2014). The approach can be seen explicitly in *Williamson*, where the judgment states that 'freedom of religion protects the subjective belief of an individual' (para 22) and was endorsed by the ECtHR in *Eweida*.

Although the courts have taken a more subjective view of belief, questions can still arise about the weight to be attached to the belief when being balanced against other rights. Here the question becomes one of whether the belief is a 'core belief', in which case it may be accorded greater protection. In *Ladele*, the domestic Court of Appeal took the view that the request not to perform civil partnerships was not a 'core' part of Ladele's religion, thus making it more ready to restrict the manifestation of that belief. However, making decisions on whether or not a belief is 'core' to the religion can lead courts into contentious theological territory. If courts are to take doctrinal matters into account in assessing religious claims, different religions or beliefs could be treated differently. Indeed, it may be that courts are more ready to determine what is and is not 'core' with regard to Christianity than other faiths. For example, at the domestic stage of the cases, in *Ladele* the Court of Appeal accepted that the belief regarding marriage was not core, and yet this can be questioned. Beliefs about marriage may or may not be 'core' to Christianity, but reframed as a belief in the authority of the bible, the question is surely central. In contrast, in cases involving other religions courts have been clear that it is not their role to determine the validity of religious views or their doctrinal status (*R (Begum) v Headteacher and Governors of Denbigh High School; R (Watkins-Singh) v The Governing Body of Aberdare Girls' High School*). An assessment of religious claims by reference to whether a belief is 'core' thus clearly has potential both to undermine the protection for religion or belief and for courts to over-step their competence (Fokas, 2015).

Another problem that arises when courts engage in an assessment of whether religious doctrine is core is that such assessments can rely on understandings of religion that are based on a binary division between inner belief and practical manifestation of that belief. As a result courts can miss some additional aspects of religious belief and practice as experienced by religious individuals, such as expressing religious or cultural identity. For example, the decision to follow a religious dress code may express religious identity as much as express a set of beliefs (Edge, 2000), and so trying to decide whether it is 'required' by the religion or not is inappropriate.

## *Theoretical underpinnings: Human rights or equality?*

A second area of difficulty faced by the courts is in achieving coherence in their treatment of religion, given the two underpinning legal frameworks on which the protection is based: human rights and equality. The two frameworks are inherently connected, both being underpinned by a concern for human dignity (Feldman, 1999), and the idea that individuals should be able to develop their own ideas of the good and exercise control over their lives (Rawls, 1999). This involves an element of respect for individual freedom of conscience and thought.

The protection of religion or belief can also be framed as an equality claim on the basis that by virtue of being human people share a fundamental right to equal concern and respect, including where they hold different conceptions of the good. Protecting religion claims for equality reasons can also be based on understandings of equality founded on notions of socioeconomic disadvantage and inclusion (Fredman, 2002), in recognition of the fact that religion and belief are at times sources of economic and social disadvantage.

The recognition that at a fundamental level human rights and equality are deeply interconnected has led to a level of improvement in the protection of each. Equality-based reasoning adds the concept of indirect discrimination and the recognition that it may be more difficult for those from religious minorities to comply with dress codes, and an appreciation of the importance of religious freedom helps balance correctly the needs of a business with the needs of the employee when it comes to uniforms.

The shared foundational roots of human rights and equality can thus serve to help courts determine the correct parameters of the law protecting religion and belief. However, the two frameworks can also be seen to be in tension. For example, in cases involving the wearing of the headscarf, some argue that religious freedom conflicts with gender equality, and in *Ladele* religious freedom and sexual orientation equality appeared to be in conflict. But here again courts will need to take care not to assume too readily that the two frameworks inevitably clash (Malik, 2008; Brems and de Lourdes Peroni Manzoni, 2015). Muslim women vary in their reasons for wearing headscarves, and Christian views on sexuality are also very varied. If courts are to correctly balance the different interests that come before them, they will need to take care to avoid essentialised views of what religious individuals believe (Modood, 1998).

## The role of religion: Public or private?

One factor that may influence the courts' treatment of claims based on religion and belief is the question of whether religion should be confined to the private sphere. Such an argument would assume work forms part of the public sphere, and that therefore restrictions on religion at work would be generally acceptable. However, a clear separation between public and private space should not be assumed when it comes to the workplace (Sandberg, 2014; Fokas, 2015). Requiring the separation of work and religion in this binary way is not a practicable option for many workers: some work is religious in nature, making separation between work and religion impossible; for many making such a separation is impracticable, for example, the *hijab* is usually worn when in the company of men who are not family members, and so has to be worn at work; others may hold the belief that all work is sacred, or may see religious witness in the everyday (Fahlbeck, 2004).

The difficulty in viewing work as only a public space has been recognised in the case law of the ECHR which has held that it is 'work ... may form part and parcel of [a person's] life to such a degree that it becomes impossible to know in what capacity he is acting at a given moment of time' (*Niemietz v Germany*, para 29). When religious practices cannot easily be separated between the home and work spheres, or indeed where work is the main forum in which the requirement arises precisely because it is not a private space, the reservation of religious observance to the world outside work amounts to a denial of the option to comply with the religious requirement.

The question of whether religious rights should extend to the work context has not been addressed directly in the UK courts as the cases arise in the context of the Equality Act that is designed to apply at work. However, the issue was addressed by the ECtHR in the case of *Eweida* (*Eweida et al v the United Kingdom*), where the Court accepted that work-based restrictions on a person's exercise of religious freedom can amount to a *prima facie* infringement of the right to freedom of religion or belief, and would need to be justified as a proportionate means of achieving a legitimate aim.

## *Hierarchy between grounds*

A common theme in the discussion about the relationship between religion or belief and equality law has been whether the law creates a hierarchy between the different protected characteristics, most usually as between religion or belief on the one hand, and sex or sexual orientation equality on the other. Religion and belief can be said to be higher in the hierarchy because of the additional exemptions that are available to religion and belief-based organisations, and in particular the exemption related to sex and sexual orientation discrimination in the appointment of clergy and other such religious personnel (see Schedule 9 of the Equality Act 2010). Conversely, it has been argued (Hambler, 2015) that religion and belief are treated less favourably than sexual orientation, with cases such as the Asher's bakery case and the *Bull v Hall* used as illustration. However, assuming that there must be a hierarchy just because in these cases one side has won or because of the creation of a special exception (Sandberg, 2014) may be to assume too readily that the courts are creating a hierarchy (Pearson, 2016).

An alternative explanation of the case law in which sexual orientation appears to have won is that rather than this reflecting a hierarchy between protected characteristics, it instead reflects a hierarchy between direct and indirect discrimination. Using the *Ladele* case as an example, the council's requirement that its registrars perform civil partnerships indirectly discriminated against Ladele, but this was justified because her refusal to perform civil partnerships would have been directly discriminatory to gay couples on grounds of their sexual orientation. In effect, then, direct discrimination is given greater protection than indirect discrimination, because of the more direct form of harm it represents.

Thus the courts are not creating a hierarchy between different grounds of equality, nor are they giving any automatic preference to one interest over another; but rather, they are taking a fact-sensitive approach, weighing all the different interests and using the concept of proportionality to achieve a degree of balance between different claims. The use of a proportionality approach to determine cases involving competing rights reflects a legal approach to theoretical problems that is based on practical solutions, reached on a case-by-case basis (Fokas, 2015) rather than on any predetermined hierarchy of rights.

## *Consistency in approach to religion or belief*

A final, broader concern relating to the legal treatment of religion and belief claims relates to questions of consistency, and whether it matters that the cases are decided similarly across Europe. The law in the UK is based on the two Europe-wide legal frameworks, the ECHR that covers the 47 member states of the Council of Europe, and EU equality law that binds the 28 member states of the European Union (EU), and yet the treatment of religion or belief is very different in the different member states. For example, Belgium and France ban headscarves and other religious symbols in the public sector; in contrast, in the UK even the police and judges can wear turbans and *hijabs* (van Ooijen, 2012). Recent cases of the ECtHR (*Eweida et al v the United Kingdom*) and the Court of Justice of the EU [CJEU] (*Achbita v G4S; Bougnaoui v Micropole*) effectively treat the religious claims in a similar way, leaving a significant amount of discretion to domestic courts, which can take into account a range of issues when deciding whether a restriction on religion is proportionate, including the national context. This allows domestic courts to take account of matters such as attitudes to church state relations and to secularity within the state when assessing whether it is proportionate to uphold restrictions on religion or belief.

The willingness of the two European Courts to allow states some discretion in their approach to religion or belief is of interest given recent moves to increase integration, both political and social, across Europe. The European Council has taken the view that 'employment is a key part of the integration process' (European Council, 2004), and the EU Equality Directives can be understood in this context. Yet the way in which both the CJEU and the ECHR allow wide differences in the treatment of religion and belief in different states seems to undermine the policy of integration.

The approach of the courts in tolerating different standards of protection across Europe is more understandable when viewed from a political perspective. As seen from the difficult debates in the drafting of the EU treaties and the development of the EU Constitution (McCrea, 2010), member states seem unwilling to accept common standards when it comes to matters of religion and belief, despite their acceptance of harmonisation on many other issues. Thus it is perhaps unsurprising that Europe's two courts have taken an approach that defers to national context when assessing religion or belief claims.

Approaching the protection of religion or belief as a matter of equality and as a matter of human rights, one might expect to have seen a greater concern to achieve some level of consistency in the legal treatment of key questions such as whether religious staff can wear religious symbols in the workplace. However, in practice, achieving a level of consistency in the legal treatment of religious claims across Europe remains a challenge.

## *The legal response: Using a proportionality framework*

This review of UK cases suggests that it can be difficult to deal adequately with the complexity that arises when law meets religion and belief. The approach of the courts has been to rely on the notion of proportionality: whether using the equality or human rights framework, the question of whether a restriction on religion or belief is acceptable is assessed by whether it is a proportionate means of achieving a legitimate aim. This allows the wide array of factual situations that arise to be treated in a nuanced manner, and for a significant range of factors to be taken into account to assess whether any proposed action is proportionate.

The proportionality approach allows distinctions to be made that reflect both the range of factual situations that arise and broader contextual matters. For example, courts can take into account practical questions such as whether anyone else is available to carry out a particular task or whether an alternative uniforms can be devised. Contextual issues can also be taken into account, such as the economic or social disadvantage that may be suffered by the religious group; any stigma attached to the religion in question; whether a restriction on the manifestation of religion at work denies the individual an opportunity to work; and issues of intersectional discrimination, such as the fact that bans on head coverings have a particular impact on Muslim women. Proportionality does not automatically mean that religion or belief will be protected or accommodated, as factors that may tell against accommodating religious practices would be weighed in the balance too: for example, an employer's interest in setting its own image or ethos, secular or religious; interests such as economic efficiency; and health and safety concerns. An approach to religion or belief claims based on proportionality retains flexibility for domestic courts, but equally helps create equilibrium between competing rights (Vickers, 2016).

## Conclusion

Formulating a coherent legal response to the inherent conflicts arising between religious interests and other interests with which religion may conflict has presented significant challenges for the courts. Courts have sometimes struggled to avoid treading on theological territory when assessing the validity of claims, and have not always been consistent in their treatment of different protected characteristics, giving rise to claims that a hierarchy is developing within equality law.

It is sometimes suggested that different legal forms would better protect religion or belief in the legal sphere, such as a right to reasonable accommodation (Alidadi, 2012). However, I would suggest that the legal model that has been developed in the UK and Europe, based on the notion of proportionality, already has the potential to adjudicate between conflicting rights, and that new legal forms are not necessary.

The protection of religion both as a matter of equality and human rights through a legal framework that relies on the notion of proportionality creates the legal space in which the full range of factors that may arise in a case, both individualised fact-sensitive matters and broader contextual factors, can be given due weight. Although the cases suggest that we are not there yet, protection based on proportionality creates the potential to develop a legal response to religion or belief in which religious interests can coexist with the rights of others as part of a broad and inclusive protection for equality and human rights.

## References

Alidadi, K. (2012) 'Reasonable accommodations for religion and belief: Adding value to Art. 9 ECHR and the European Union's anti-discrimination approach to employment?', *European Law Review*, vol 37, no 6, pp 693-713.

Brems, E. and de Lourdes Peroni Manzoni, M. (2015) 'Religion and human rights: Deconstructing and navigating tensions' in S. Ferrari (ed) *Routledge handbook of law and religion*, London: Routledge, pp 145-59.

Cumper, P. (2001) 'The public manifestation of religion or belief: Challenges for a multi-faith society in the twenty-first century', in A. Lewis and R. O'Dair (eds) *Current legal issues*, vol 4, Oxford: Oxford University Press, pp 311-28.

Edge, P.W. (2000) 'Religious rights and choice under the European Convention on Human Rights', *Web Journal of Current Legal Issues*.

European Council (2004) *Common basic principles for immigrant integration policy in the European Union*, Council document 14615/04, 19.11.2004, agreed by the European Council.

Fahlbeck, R. (2004) 'Ora et Labora on freedom of religion at the work place: A stakeholder cum balancing factors model', *The International Journal of Comparative Labour Law and Industrial Relations*, vol 20, no 1, pp 27-64.

Feldman, D. (1999) 'Human dignity as a legal value: Part 1', *Public Law*, pp 682-702.

Fokas, E. (2015) 'Sociology at the intersection between law and religion', in S. Ferrari (ed) *Routledge handbook of law and religion*, London: Routledge, pp 59-74.

Fredman, S. (2002) *The future of equality in Britain*, EOC Working Paper Series No 5, London: Equal Opportunities Commission.

Hambler, A. (2015) *Religious expression in the workplace and the contested role of law*, London: Routledge.

Hill, D.J. and Whistler, D. (2013) 'Religious symbols and the European Convention on Human Rights', *Law and Justice*, vol 52, issue 171, pp 52-69.

Malik, M. (2008) '"From conflict to cohesion": Competing interests in equality law and policy', Paper for the Equality and Diversity Forum (www.edf.org.uk/wp-content/uploads/2009/02/competing-rigts-report_web.pdf).

McCrea, R. (2010) *Religion and the public order of the European Union*, Oxford: Oxford University Press.

Mitchell, M. and Beninger, K. with Howard, E. and Donald, A. (2015) *Religion or belief in the workplace and service delivery*, Manchester: Equality and Human Rights Commission (www.equalrightstrust.org/ertdocumentbank/RoB%20Call%20for%20Evidence%20Report.pdf).

Modood, T. (1998) 'Anti-essentialism, multiculturalism and the "recognition" of religious groups', *Journal of Political Philosophy*, vol 6, no 4, pp 378-99.

Pearson, M. (2016) 'Religious discrimination and the "hierarchy of rights": Non-existent, appropriate or problematic?', *International Journal of Discrimination and the Law*, vol 16, no 1, pp 37-50.

Rawls, J. (1999) *A theory of justice* (revised edn), Oxford: Oxford University Press.

Sandberg, R. (2014) *Religion, law and society*, Cambridge: Cambridge University Press.

van Ooijen, H. (2012) *Religious symbols in public functions: Unveiling state neutrality. A comparative analysis of Dutch, English and French justifications for limiting the freedom of public officials to display religious symbols*, Antwerp: Intersentia.

Vickers, L. (2016) *Religious freedom, religious discrimination and the workplace* (2nd edn), Oxford: Hart Publishing.

### Case law

*Achbita v G4S Case C-157/15, judgment of 14 March 2017*
*Arrowsmith v UK [1978] 3 EHRR 218*
*Azmi v Kirklees Metropolitan Borough Council [2007] ICR 1154*

*Bougnaoui v Micropole Case C-188/15, judgment of 14 March 2017*
*Bull & Anor v Hall & Anor [2013] UKSC 73*
*Eweida et al v the United Kingdom [2013] 57 EHRR 213*
*Ladele v Islington Borough Council [2009] EWCA Civ 1357; then heard with Eweida (Applications nos 48420/10, 59842/10, 51671/10 and 36516/10) Judgment 15 January 2013*
*Lee v McArthur & Ors [2016] NICA 29*
*Niemietz v Germany [1992] 16 EHRR 7, para 29*
*R (Begum) v Headteacher and Governors of Denbigh High School [2006] UKHL 15*
*R (Watkins-Singh) v The Governing Body of Aberdare Girls' High School [2008] EWHC 1865 (Admin)*
*R v Secretary of State for Education and Employment and others ex parte Williamson [2005] UKHL 15, para 22*

# SIX

# Reading religion through the lessons of legal decisions and reactions to them

Lori G. Beaman

## Introduction

The new diversity is presenting some important challenges for social scientists that require a recalibration of our tools. By new diversity I mean that the religious landscape has changed, prompted first by increased immigration that is bringing greater numbers of people whose religious practices are not confined to the majoritarian religions of the receiving countries (see Vertovec, 2007; Meissner and Vertovec, 2014; for a critique of these ideas, see Crul, 2016). Often this is accompanied by a fear of that 'other', who is frequently, although not always, Muslim. Second, majoritarian religions are rapidly transforming, losing members, for example, and experiencing declining attendance and participation in life rituals. At the same time, majoritarian religions are refashioning themselves as culture and heritage. Third, in some countries (especially Canada, Australia, the US and some countries in Latin America) this new diversity also includes a renewed attention to indigenous peoples and their spiritualities. In Canada, which is the country I am most familiar with, this attention is part of an awareness of the need to acknowledge the brutal legacy of colonisation for indigenous peoples. Finally, and related to the second shift, is the growing number of people who self-identify as non-religious. All of these changes are shifts in degree rather than kind, but together they constitute a changing landscape in relation to religion. These transformations are resulting in increasingly complex societies that require trans- and interdisciplinary approaches to understand them.

As a scholar who is trained in Sociology and Law (and who is located in a department of Religious Studies) I am interested in how law imagines religion and its position in society. I am, following Beckford (2003), a moderate social constructionist, which means that I am not so much interested in what religion or non-religion are, or how they are defined, but in how they are constructed and imagined by social actors and social institutions. Legal cases often reveal a great deal about the process of that construction and what is at stake in the various configurations of religion. They draw our attention away from strictly academic definitions of, and debates about, religion, and offer a glimpse into policy and politics. Moreover, legal cases offer a window into very real tensions and issues in everyday life: issues such as the fight to take assisted dying out of the moral domain of Christianity, the issue of prayer before council meetings, the wearing of a *niqab* in court and during such things as citizenship ceremonies all reflect intense discussions about what is configured as religion in the public sphere and who decides. Not every landmark issue or debate makes it to court, and in fact it would be nice to think that most don't. But contentious issues that are settled by the courts offer a detailed record of how social actors present themselves and the 'other' in relation to religion.

For the purposes of this chapter I explore three ways to think about law and religion that might bear fruit in terms of revealing new developments, past lessons and what is on the horizon in the context of this new diversity regarding thinking about religion and society: (1) From the point of view of subject matter: what, if anything, is new in the sorts of cases we see coming before the courts? (2) How is law conceptualising religion – has it changed? And (3) how does law contextualise religion – what are religions' 'relationships' as imagined by law? I focus primarily on Canada, but the discussion is relevant beyond the Canadian context, and I would therefore invite you, the reader, to reflect on these themes in relation to your own country.

## Subject matter

A scan of the Supreme Court of Canada decisions on religion reveals a range of topics that broadly coalesce around the subject areas of education (*The Queen v Jones; Loyola High School v Quebec*), religious symbols and the public sphere (*Mouvement laïque québécois v Saguenay [City]; R v NS; Syndicat Northcrest v Amselem*) and religious practices and their 'exemption' (*Alberta v Hutterian Brethren of Wilson Colony; Multani v Commission scolaire Marguerite-Bourgeoys; R v Big M Drug Mart Ltd; R v Brooks*), with variations on themes that sometimes take courts into territory they claim not to be in, which is the adjudication of the content of religion, or put otherwise, proper theology or practice. Courts sidestep this issue by focusing on the sincerity of the believer (or claimant) rather than whether the practice in question is authentically part of a given tradition. I have argued elsewhere, however, that it is impossible for courts to actually do this, that is, to completely avoid the adjudication of theology and practice (Beaman, 2008) – that is, what it means to be Catholic or Jewish when one is making legal claims based on those identity categories.

Is there anything new in the topics the courts are considering related to religion that might seem to respond to the new diversity? Religion and education has long been a subject of adjudication in the courts in Canada – prayer in schools, the regulation of religious schools, the funding of schools, gay and lesbian students in religious schools, curriculum content and religious objection have all come before the courts. Although there are interesting variations on the themes, law has a long history of adjudicating matters related to religion and education and religion in the public sphere.

Is the focus on religious symbols and the spatial organisation of religion a new development? Again, there are interesting variations on the theme of which religious group can do what in public space, but these issues have come up previously in Canadian law (and elsewhere). For example, pre-Charter cases, that is, those prior *to* Part I of the Constitution Act 1982, or more commonly known as the Canadian Charter of Rights and Freedoms (the Charter), include 121 cases in Quebec which dealt with Jehovah's Witnesses and their presence in public parks as well as their right to evangelise door-to-door, the best known being *Roncarelli v Duplessis* and *Saumur v City of Quebec*. The current primary focus of debates about religion in the public sphere is focused on Muslim women and their clothing. Perhaps the best known case is that of *Ishaq v Canada (Citizenship and Immigration)*, in which the Federal Court overturned the then Conservative government's ban against the wearing of face coverings during the oath of allegiance at Canadian citizenship ceremonies. Even the former Prime Minister, Stephen Harper, weighed in, saying 'why would Canadians, contrary to our own values, embrace a practice rooted at that time that is not transparent, that is not open and, frankly, is rooted in a culture that is anti-women that is unacceptable to Canadians, unacceptable'? (quoted in CBC News, 2015). The Prime Minister, an evangelical Christian, seemed to have become an expert on Islam and Muslim opinion, noting 'Muslim women are not obligated, not required to cover their faces in public' and 'most moderate Muslims support the ban' (quoted in CBC News, 2015). But before Muslims it was Sikhs and kirpans (see *Multani v Commission scolaire Marguerite-Bourgeoys*) and turbans (*Grant v Canada [Attorney General]*). So, although contentious and sometimes heated, religious symbols and practices have consistently attracted legal attention.

## Definition of religion

Perhaps more interesting is the way in which courts are defining religion. Like all of us, courts have struggled to define religion, embracing both substantive (what is religion) and functional (what does religion do) approaches. An early post-Charter pronouncement by Justice Dickson in the *Big M Drug Mart* case gives some hints as to how the courts understood religion:

I would like to stress that nothing in these reasons should be read as suggesting any opposition to Sunday being spent as a religious day; quite the contrary. It is recognized that for a great number of Canadians, Sunday is the day when their souls rest in God, when the spiritual takes priority over the material, a day which, to them, gives security and meaning because it is linked to Creation and the Creator. It is a day which brings a balanced perspective to life, an opportunity for man to be in communion with man and with God. In my view, however, as I read the Charter, it mandates that the legislative preservation of a Sunday day of rest should be secular, the diversity of belief and non-belief, the diverse socio-cultural backgrounds of Canadians make it constitutionally incompetent for the federal Parliament to provide legislative preference for any one religion at the expense of those of another religious persuasion.

In an earlier time, when people believed in the collective responsibility of the community toward some deity, the enforcement of religious conformity may have been a legitimate object of government, but since the Charter, it is no longer legitimate. With the Charter, it has become the right of every Canadian to work out for himself or herself what his or her religious obligations, if any, should be and it is not for the state to dictate otherwise. The state shall not use the criminal sanctions at its disposal to achieve a religious purpose, namely, the uniform observance of the day chosen by the Christian religion as its day of rest. (*Big M Drug Mart*, para 134-5)

The first paragraph introduces a rather romantic notion of religious life, 'man communing with man and god'. The Court here recounts a former time of collective engagement, and then introduces a very individualistic narrative about how religion works, implicitly accepting a simplistic secularisation thesis that moves from sacred canopy (Berger and Luckmann, 1966; Berger, 1967) to Sheilaism (Bellah, 1985).

In Canada, the *Amselem* case is widely recognised to have marked a shift in how the Supreme Court conceptualised religion. Although characterised as moving to a purely subjective understanding of religion that considered only the sincerity of belief of the claimant, this is a simplistic read of the Court's approach, which, despite holding that experts were not necessary to establish the parameters of religions and the authenticity of practices as 'really' religious, still required some connection to the believer and the religion. The Court emphasised sincerity, rather than content, of belief in its assessment of the claim, and it was this emphasis that formed the basis of the characterisation of the case as a turn to a purely subjective understanding of religion. The costs of this formulation were borne by the *Hutterian Brethren* in a later case when they tried to argue that they should be exempt from a requirement to have their photographs on their driver's licences on religious grounds:

> However, in many cases, the incidental effects of a law passed for the general good on a particular religious practice may be less serious. The limit may impose costs on the religious practitioner in terms of money, tradition or inconvenience. However, these costs may still leave the adherent with a meaningful choice concerning the religious practice at issue. (*Hutterian Brethren*, para 95)

> Many businesses and individuals rely on hired persons and commercial transport for their needs, either because they cannot drive or choose not to drive. Obtaining alternative transport would impose an additional economic cost on the Colony, and would go against their traditional self-sufficiency. But there is no evidence that this would be prohibitive. (*Hutterian Brethren*, para 97)

In what might be seem as a move away from the individualistic emphasis in *Amselem*, the Supreme Court in 2015 also expressly recognised the communal aspects of religion in the *Loyola* case:

> The communal character of religion means that protecting the religious freedom of individuals requires protecting the

> religious freedom of religious organizations, including religious educational bodies such as Loyola. (*Loyola*, para 91)

> The individual and collective aspects of freedom of religion are indissolubly intertwined. The freedom of religion of individuals cannot flourish without freedom of religion for the organizations through which those individuals express their religious practices and through which they transmit their faith. (*Loyola*, para 94)

The possible return to a collective understanding of religion signals a shift to a more traditional understanding of religion. This move raises some interesting questions about an emerging tension between two narratives regarding what is occurring in particularly Western democracies: one narrative tells the story of the return of religion, largely understood as institutional, collective, communal religion, and the other tells the story of the move away from institutional religion to a more individualistic, subjective, lived model that increasingly also includes the choice to have no religion at all.

Most recently the Court grappled with indigenous religion in the *Ktunaxa Nation v British Columbia* decision. In that case the Ktunaxa sought to stop a ski resort development on land inhabited by the Grizzly Bear Spirit. They argued that the resort would cause the Spirit to leave, which would destroy their religious practice and community. Although the Court recognised the communal nature of religion, it also limited it by restricting its protection if it had an impact on others who did not share their beliefs. The Court was of the opinion that the Ktunaxa were asking it to protect not just their beliefs, but also the object of their beliefs, in this case, the Grizzly Bear Spirit. The Court used the word 'spiritual' and religious almost interchangeably, and said that its use of the word 'spiritual' tracked the wording of the submission by the Ktunaxa:

> In this analysis we employ the term "spiritual" rather than "religious" only because this term was used by the parties in their submissions. As the chambers judge rightly noted (at para 275),

there is no issue here that the Ktunaxa's system of spiritual beliefs constitutes a religion. (*Ktunaxa Nation*, para 89)

The Court had no issue with bringing the spiritual under the protection of freedom of religion. Although there is much to say about this case, for the purposes here it is this small mention of spirituality that is pertinent to our discussion of the definition of religion. It also seems that the Court put a strong emphasis on belief rather than practice in the decision, a move that may be a reversion to a more Christian understanding of religion. Unfortunately, although reconciliation with indigenous peoples was mentioned in the decision, this did not translate into placing the needs of the Ktunaxa above commercial development of an area that is spiritually central to them.

If social scientists and humanities scholars have failed to define religion in any definitive way, and I think they have, it is hardly likely that law will be successful. Instead, we might ask (and I frankly think that this is the more interesting question), what is the work that the definitions chosen by law are doing? What are the power relations embedded in them, what privilege attaches to being 'religious' or 'culture', and how do certain definitions exclude particular groups or people and include others? Sometimes the definition may be driven by practical concerns: in *Amselem*, a case involving the placement of a *succah* on the balcony of a condominium building that explicitly prohibited structures on balconies, there was conflicting evidence about what, precisely, was mandatory in relation to *succahs* and the festival of *Succot*. Was one, for example, required to have one's own *succah*? The problem of the rabbis' conflicting evidence who were expert witnesses was solved by introducing the idea of sincerely held belief. In other words, it didn't matter if the practice fits precisely within a canon that could be identified by an expert:

[R]egardless of the position taken by religious officials and in religious texts, provided that an individual demonstrates that he or she sincerely believes that a certain practice or belief is experientially religious in nature in that it is either objectively

> required by the religion, *or* that he or she subjectively believes that it is required by the religion, *or* that he or she sincerely believes that the practice engenders a personal, subjective connection to the divine or to the subject or object of his or her spiritual faith, and as long as that practice has a nexus with religion, it should trigger the protection of s. 3 of the Quebec Charter or that of s. 2 (a) of the Canadian Charter, or both, depending on the context. (*Amselem*, para 69)

What mattered was that the practitioner sincerely believed that the practice was part of his or her religion. This, in turn, happens to mesh quite nicely with the 'lived religion' approach in Sociology as articulated by Meredith McGuire (2008), Linda Woodhead (2011) and Nancy T. Ammerman (2014).

## Religion's relationships

An examination of subject matter and definitions lend limited insight into shifts in law that reveal a re-imagining of religion in the 21st century. Perhaps the most significant observation is that law has moved more toward a subjective turn in understanding religion, akin to Sociology's more enthusiastic embracing of lived religion. However, a focus on religion's relationships and law's conceptualisation of those produces a more comprehensive picture of the major battles and fault lines that surround religion in the future and the new diversity introduced at the beginning of this chapter. The *Saguenay* case illustrates some of these relationships.

In 2007 the *Mouvement Laïque Québécois* (Quebec Secular Movement), on behalf of Alain Simoneau, filed a complaint with the Quebec Human Rights Commission (*Commission des droits de la personne et des droits de la jeunesse* [CDPDJ]). Simoneau, a self-identified atheist, noted that prior to council meetings in the City of Saguenay the mayor made the sign of the cross, stated 'In the name of the Father, the Son and the Holy Spirit' and then recited a prayer. Simoneau also pointed out that the council room contained a rather large crucifix (over two feet high, a foot wide and five inches thick) and a sacred heart statue of similar dimensions that was displayed in an elevated position on the wall.

The case went to the Human Rights Tribunal (*Simoneau v Tremblay*, hereinafter *Saguenay Tribunal*), which heard evidence on a range of subjects, including the nature of the statue, the crucifix and the prayer:

> Almighty God, we thank You for the many favours that You have granted Saguenay and its citizens, including freedom, opportunities for development and peace. Guide us in our deliberations as members of the municipal council and help us to be well aware of our duties and responsibilities. Grant us the wisdom, knowledge and understanding that will enable us to preserve the advantages that our city enjoys, so that everyone can benefit from them and we can make wise decisions. Amen. (*Saguenay Tribunal*, para 28)

The City argued that these were not in fact religious, but reflective of culture and heritage, and that the state therefore had a duty to protect them. Simoneau argued that they were religious and had no place in a municipal council meeting. The Tribunal found that the prayer and the artefacts had religious meaning, and that

> The reciting of a prayer and the exhibiting of religious symbols in the state-controlled space constituted by the meetings of the municipal council, where representatives of the people discuss questions of public interest, also have a non-trivial exclusionary effect that substantially stigmatizes people who do not share those values. (*Saguenay Tribunal*, para 251)

The City of Saguenay appealed, and in 2013 the matter went to the Quebec Court of Appeal (*Saguenay [Ville de] v Mouvement laïque Québécois*, hereinafter *Saguenay CA*), which accepted the argument that the prayer and artefacts were not really religious, that they were cultural and of heritage value, that the state could not be neutral on this matter, that the expert called by the Mouvement Laïque and Mr Simoneau was not a reliable expert, and that any harm to Mr Simoneau was trivial. The Court of Appeal relied on the *Lautsi* decision (*Lautsi and others v Italy*) from the European Court of Human Rights Grand Chamber to support the idea of the cultural and heritage value of the prayer, crucifix and statue and the universality of the values those represent. In contrast, the Supreme Court of Canada (*Mouvement laïque québécois v Saguenay [City]*, hereinafter *Saguenay SCC*) ruled, focusing on the prayer, that 'if the state adheres to a form of religious expression under the guise of cultural or historical reality or heritage, it breaches its duty of neutrality' (*Saguenay SCC*, para 78).

The Supreme Court decision and the decisions that preceded it reveal some interesting developments around religion in the new diversity. First, majoritarian religion is being transformed into culture and heritage; second, courts are considering religion in the context of state ideology about the good society (in the case of Canada, this often invokes multiculturalism – in France, for example, it is '*vivre ensemble*'); and finally, the relationship between religion and the state requires a clear articulation that is imagined as neutrality.

## *Religion to culture*

The idea that majoritarian religion should be protected under the 'guise' of culture and heritage, to use the word of the Supreme Court of Canada, is an emerging trend in law and simultaneously in public discussion. Although a number of cases have seen this type of argument made (for example, *Otto-Preminger-Institut v Austria*), the *Lautsi* case was specifically relied on in *Saguenay* at the Court of Appeal level. The European Court of Human Rights Grand Chamber entertained this argument in relation to a crucifix on a classroom wall. Justice Bonello commented as follows:

> A court of human rights cannot allow itself to suffer from historical Alzheimer's. It has no right to disregard the cultural continuum of a nation's flow through time, nor to ignore what,

over the centuries, has served to mould and define the profile of a people. No supranational court has any business substituting its own ethical mock-ups for those qualities that history has imprinted on the national identity. On a human rights court falls the function of protecting fundamental rights, but never ignoring that "customs are not passing whims. They evolve over time, harden over history into cultural cement. They become defining, all-important badges of identity for nations, tribes, religions, individuals". (Justice Bonello, in *Lautsi*, p 38, 1.1)

The European Court's decision validated the possibility of a transformation of religion into culture and heritage and feeds back into a public discourse that picks up this same characterisation. Moreover, however, it imagined this space of culture and heritage as being 'outside of the law' and untouchable, almost (ironically) 'sacred':

A European court should not be called upon to bankrupt centuries of European tradition. No court, certainly not this Court, should rob the Italians of part of their cultural personality. (Justice Bonello, in *Lautsi*, p.38, 1.2)

The interesting question that results from the *Lautsi* case and others like it is when, how and by whom symbols and practices are constituted as being 'religious' or 'culture and heritage'. In other words, under what circumstances is religion constructed as religion, and when is it transformed into culture and heritage?

The idea that symbols and practices that have traditionally had religious meaning are indisputable artefacts of culture and heritage represents a broader trend in Western democracies to exempt majoritarian religion from legal scrutiny. Most of these regimes have constitutional protections of religious freedom and some sense that states should not favour one religion over another. However, by situating majoritarian religion as culture, the state can justify protecting majoritarian religious practices and artefacts. Indeed, the state is called to protect practices and symbols that exemplify the nation's culture and heritage. The situation is particularly complex because of the decline in religiosity – despite participation in majoritarian religion, there remains a strong attachment to the religious past, often as part of a nationalist project, although that, too, is complicated (Zubrzycki, 2006). The lack of participation does not translate into an absence of identification with majoritarian religion. Moreover, this new version of religion as culture and heritage is validated as essential to the moral fabric of the nation. Those who challenge such 'cultural' practices and symbols are characterised as unreasonable, radical and even as having psychiatric problems. In the *Saguenay* case, the Tribunal stated:

> He [the expert] could not see how the reciting of the prayer could have a negative cognitive impact other than minimal inconvenience on a non-believer. Rather, to claim that the municipal council prayer prejudices a non-believer would be indicative of a problem of a [TRANSLATION] "neuropsychological or psychiatric" kind. (*Saguenay Tribunal*, para 174)

Although law is a key collaborator and perhaps even a driver of the transmutation of majoritarian religion into culture, in this instance the Supreme Court of Canada did not accept the argument that the religious practice in question could be justified on the grounds that it is really culture and heritage. The Court did, however, leave open the possibility that such an argument could work in the future, but went on to say:

> This being said, it must be recognized that the Canadian cultural landscape includes many traditional and heritage practices that are religious in nature. Although it is clear that not all of these cultural expressions are in breach of the state's duty of neutrality, there is also no doubt that the state may not consciously make a profession of faith or act so as to adopt or favour one religious view at the expense of all others. (*Saguenay SCC*, para 87)

And

> Tradition cannot be used to justify such a use of public powers. (*Saguenay SCC*, para 118)

What does this reveal about religion in the 21st century? As traditionally majoritarian religions lose ground in terms of tangible participation, they are constituting themselves as culture and heritage. Rather than being one religion (or non-religion) among many, they retain a privileged status as culture and heritage that becomes unassailable and inextricably linked to citizenship. Cases such as *Saguenay* illuminate the contours of this shift and the sorts of arguments being used to re-affirm the place of majoritarian religion as culture.

## *Religion and multiculturalism*

Religion's relationship to defining narratives of who 'we' are is also being articulated in case law. In the example of Canada, multiculturalism has been one of those narratives for the past 50 years. In *Saguenay* the Supreme Court reflected on the relationship of religion and multiculturalism. This is not the first time it has done so, but in *Saguenay* there are some new developments that tangle together religion, spirituality, freedom of conscience and multiculturalism into a new knot that forms part of the tapestry of Canadian identity. The Court said:

> [A] neutral public space free from coercion, pressure and judgment on the part of public authorities in matters of spirituality is intended to protect every person's freedom and dignity. The neutrality of the public space therefore helps preserve and promote the multicultural nature of Canadian society.... (*Saguenay SCC*, para 74)

Canadians like to think they invented multiculturalism: Section 27 of the Charter states 'this Charter shall be interpreted in a manner consistent with the preservation and enhancement of the multicultural heritage of Canadians.' Such sentiments are entrenched into Canadian life by a range of social institutions, including being taught in schools. In his research on atheists in Ottawa, Canada, Steven Tomlins (2016) asked his study participants whether they had a difficult time expressing their atheism in public. Interestingly, a number of them referred to multiculturalism as the explanation for why they felt atheism was not negatively viewed in Canada. What is important to pay attention to here is how religion is positioned in relation to a national imaginary. When courts talk about religion, what do they also say about who Italians are, who Canadians are, who the French are and so on, and then, how does that fold back into religion, or is religion folded back into the national imaginary in some way? Sometimes this narrative can act as a counterbalance to the insistence that majoritarian religion is a precious heritage that must be protected by the state. This is a reasonable interpretation of what happened at the Supreme Court in the *Saguenay* case. In other cases, the narrative of who 'we' are works in tandem with the portrayal of majoritarian symbols as heritage and culture. The *Lautsi* decision might be understood as an illustration of this.

## Religion and the state

The third relationship that is important to consider when thinking about religion in the 21st century is that between religion and the state. The dominant rhetoric is one of neutrality, and indeed the Supreme Court emphasises the duty of the state to remain neutral, as we saw in the quotation above, where the Court links a neutral public space to the thriving of multiculturalism. This discussion of state neutrality vis-à-vis religion is somewhat new. Canada doesn't have a constitutional separation of church and state; indeed, there is a great deal of intermingling of religion and state including a preamble in the Charter that recognises the supremacy of God. Interestingly, the Court says of the preamble:

> The reference to the supremacy of God in the preamble to the Canadian Charter cannot lead to an interpretation of freedom of

conscience and religion that authorizes the state to consciously profess a theistic faith. The preamble, including its reference to God, articulates the "political theory" on which the *Charter's* protections are based.... (*Saguenay SCC*, para 147)

The Court also stated that the state's duty of neutrality 'does not require it to abstain from celebrating and preserving its religious heritage. But that cannot justify the state engaging in a discriminatory practice for religious purposes, which is what happened in the case of the City's prayer' (*Saguenay SCC*, para 116).

Winnifred Sullivan and I have previously argued that every state has an established religion; it is just a matter of sorting out what it is and how it regulates religion in society (Beaman and Sullivan, 2013). One of the major challenges of arriving at neutrality is that because Canada (and many other Western democracies) has so long been dominated by Christianity, its institutions have been significantly shaped by that reality. Thus, achieving neutrality is rather difficult. This does not mean that it should not be a goal. Nor does it mean that all signs of Christianity should be erased from public space. However, the new diversity calls for a renegotiation of the privilege of majoritarian religion. This is proving rather difficult in some instances and is an ongoing process, as we shall see in the next section.

## New diversity on the ground

If we move outside of the specific confines of the *Saguenay* case itself and look at the reaction to it in Canadian society, it is clear that the case reveals a gap in legal imaginary and community practice. Indeed, the unintended consequences of the case are the most fascinating part of it. In the aftermath of *Saguenay*, what became apparent was that in a so-called secular country, many municipalities were saying very Christian prayers prior to their council meetings. And these prayers were being said not only in 'Catholic Quebec', but also in a wide range of municipalities, both small and large. And some municipalities were defiant – they would continue to say the Lord's Prayer, or another prayer even in the face of the decision. Others said they would instead have a moment of silence. One day I happened to be listening to the radio the day after the motion to end the prayer and have a moment of reflection was passed in Fredericton, New Brunswick. The news report recounted some of the discussion of the councillors, some feeling that a 'moment of reflection' was not enough because people could think about anything. In other words, there was a strong desire that everyone be engaged in a Christian prayer, or in a prayer that was ostensibly universal but practically Christian. The legal case reflects back and reveals that a practice that many assumed had long ago ceased was still going strong.

On the ground, at the local level, majoritarian religion is quite present – no matter what church attendance figures might suggest and however much there are increased numbers of religious minorities. This is all the more interesting when brought into conversation with the claim that religion has been 'banished' into the private sphere. Yet, law tells a bit of a different story. What voice does religion have, for example, in major cases on religion in Canada, and perhaps more importantly, in cases with wider reach: even broader, and I think more telling, if we consider cases like *Reference re Same-Sex Marriage*, the recent *Carter v Canada* decision on assisted death, and much earlier decision on abortion in the *R v Morgentaler* case. A review of the interveners in these cases reveals a strong voice for religion. Interveners in Supreme Court cases must have leave by the Court. This means that the Court thinks they have something worthwhile to say, or that they are a voice that could be absent otherwise. In the 2015 *Carter* case on assisted death, there were 26 interveners (rather large compared to the earlier 'assisted suicide' case of *Rodriguez v British Columbia*, of which five of the nine were religious). Twelve (one not conservative), or nearly half, of the interveners were religious groups or groups with religious affiliations, including, for example, the Christian Medical and Dental Society of Canada as well as the Evangelical Fellowship of Canada. On the *Reference re Same-Sex Marriage*, there were 27 intervener submissions – 13 were religious (two not conservative). *Chamberlain v Surrey School District*, which involved a dispute over the inclusion of books that 'featured' same-sex parents in the curriculum of a British Columbia school board, had 10 interveners, 4 of which were religious. *Saguenay* had 7 interveners, 5 religious. *Loyola* had 16, all but 2 religious. Law provides another window on the claim that religious has been 'banished'. On the contrary, it seems religion, especially conservative Christian religion, has a strong voice in Supreme Court cases.

The new diversity is shaping the legal landscape in interesting ways and the law is returning the favour. I like to think that this is a reciprocal relationship as opposed to the domination of one or the other realm, although I know there are compelling arguments regarding the shadow effects of law (see Fokas, 2017). The content of religion is becoming less important than the fact that a person 'sincerely believes' that the belief or practice in question is religious or necessary to connect with the divine. The new diversity is also creating a push back that is manifesting in the transformation of majoritarian religion to culture, which in turn exempts it from the scrutiny placed on it as religion. This status as culture (and heritage) has an impact on the state's credibility in relation to neutrality. In this sense the link between the effective functioning of multiculturalism, which at its best facilitates an inclusive society, and the neutrality of the state is extremely important. The authority of traditional religion is shifting, although by no means is it disappearing. As a somewhat conservative institution itself, law is caught between protecting vulnerable groups (both religious and non-religious) such as minority religions, and defending the majoritarian religious culture within which it has been created.

## Acknowledgements

I would like to acknowledge the continued financial support for research through my Canada Research Chair in Religious Diversity and Social Change. In addition, thank you to Emily McCallum and Cory Steele for their research assistance and to Cory Steele for his editorial assistance.

## References

Ammerman, N.T. (2014) 'Finding religion in everyday life', *Sociology of Religion*, vol 75, no 2, pp 189-207.

Beaman, L.G. (2008) 'Defining religion: The promise and the perils of legal interpretation', in R. Moon (ed) *Law and religious pluralism in Canada*, Vancouver: UBC Press, pp 192-216.

Beaman, L.G. and Sullivan, W.F. (2013) 'Neighbo(u)rly misreadings and misconstruals: A cross-border conversation', in W.F. Sullivan and L.G. Beaman (eds) *Varieties of religious establishment*, Farnham: Ashgate, pp 1-11.

Beckford, J.A. (2003) *Social theory and religion*, Cambridge: Cambridge University Press.

Bellah, R.N. (1985) *Habits of the heart: Individualism and commitment in American life*, Berkeley, CA: University of California Press.

Berger, P. (1967) *The sacred canopy: Elements of a sociological theory of religion*, New York: Doubleday & Company.

Berger, P. and Luckmann, T. (1966) *The social construction of reality: A treatise in the sociology of knowledge*, Garden City, NY: Doubleday.

CBC News (2015) 'Will Stephen Harper regret remark on niqabs?', 12 March (www.cbc.ca/news/canada/manitoba/will-stephen-harper-regret-remark-on-niqabs-1.2991721).

Crul, M. (2016) 'Super-diversity vs. assimilation: How complex diversity in majority-minority cities challenges the assumptions of assimilation', *Journal of Ethnic and Migration Studies*, vol 42, no 1, pp 54-68.

Fokas, E. (2017) 'The European Court of Human Rights at the grassroots level: Who knows what about religion at the ECtHR and to what effects?', *Religion, State and Society*, vol 45, no 3-4, pp 249-67.

McGuire, M.B. (2008) *Lived religion: Faith and practice in everyday life*, Oxford: Oxford University Press.

Meissner, F. and Vertovec, S. (2014) 'Comparing super-diversity', *Ethnic and Racial Studies*, vol 38, no 4, pp 541-55.

Tomlins, S. (2016) Navigating atheist identities: An analysis of nonreligious perceptions and experiences in the religiously diverse Canadian city of Ottawa', PhD thesis, University of Ottawa.

Vertovec, S. (2007) 'Super-diversity and its implications', *Ethnic and Racial Studies*, vol 30, no 6, pp 1024-54.

Woodhead, L. (2011) 'Five concepts of religion', *International Review of Sociology*, vol 21, no 1, pp 121-43.

Zubrzycki, G. (2006) *The crosses of Auschwitz: Nationalism and religion in post-communist Poland*, Chicago, IL: University of Chicago Press.

## Case law

*Alberta v Hutterian Brethren of Wilson Colony* [2009] SCC 37, [2009] 2 SCR 567

*Carter v Canada (Attorney General)* [2015] SCC 5, [2015] 1 SCR 331

*Chamberlain v Surrey School District No 36* [2002] 4 SCR 710, [2002] SCC 86

*Grant v Canada (Attorney General) (TD)* [1995] 1 FC 158

*Ishaq v Canada (Citizenship and Immigration)* [2015] 4 FCR 297, [2015] FC 156

*Ktunaxa Nation v British Columbia (Forests, Lands and Natural Resource Operations)* [2017] SCC 54

*Lautsi and others v Italy* [2011] ECHR No 30814/06

*Loyola High School v Quebec (Attorney General)* [2015] SCC 12, [2015] 1 SCR 613

*Mouvement laïque québécois v Saguenay (City)* [2015] SCC 16, [2015] 2 SCR 3

*Multani v Commission scolaire Marguerite-Bourgeoys* [2006] 1 SCR 256, [2006] SCC 6

*Otto-Preminger-Institut v Austria*, (13470/87) [1994] ECHR 26

*R v Big M Drug Mart Ltd* [1985] 1 SCR 295

*R v Brooks* [2000] 1 SCR 237

*R v Morgentaler* [1988] 1 SCR

*R v NS* [2012] SCC 72, [2012] 3 SCR 726

*Reference re Same-Sex Marriage* [2004] 3 SCR 698, [2004] SCC 79

*Rodriguez v British Columbia (Attorney General)* [1993] 3 SCR 519

*Roncarelli v Duplessis* [1959] SCR 121

*Saguenay (Ville de) v Mouvement laïque québécois* [2013] QCCA 936

*Saumur v City of Quebec* [1953] 2 SCR 299

*Simoneau v Tremblay* [2011] QCTDP 1

*Syndicat Northcrest v Amselem* [2004] 2 SCR 551, 2004 SCC 47

*The Queen v Jones* [1986] 2 SCR 284

# SEVEN

# Religious dimensions of postcolonial policy in Australia

Mark G. Brett

## Introduction

Over the past decade, Jürgen Habermas has provoked a conversation about some fundamental questions in public discourse. In the wake of numerous terrorist incidents, he has interrogated the polarisation of worldviews that splits societies into religious and secular camps. Habermas identified the need for a 'postsecular' discourse within which religious and secular contributions can learn from each other, and forge the solidarities that are necessary if violence is to be avoided. Although he suggested that fundamentalism in some parts of the world may reflect 'failures in decolonization' (Habermas, 2006, p 1), he has confessed in another context that his own proposals may not be readily applicable in settler colonial contexts. He seems to suggest that Indigenous cultures might need to be considered 'external to egalitarian law' in Western societies like the US, Canada and Australia (Habermas, 2008, pp 304-5). This chapter investigates some of the 'failures in decolonisation' in Australia, and also considers new opportunities that may be enabled by postsecular discourse. I argue that a political ethic of reconciliation focused on restorative justice can be informed by a variety of religious traditions, and that such a political ethic can address the gaps created by utilitarian policies.

Along with Habermas, we may acknowledge at the outset that there is no easy way to integrate Indigenous cultures within democratic systems of government. The utilitarian norms that embrace the wellbeing of the majority, and which commonly underpin democratic arrangements, are manifestly inadequate when it comes to the protection of minority interests. Similarly, policies designed to address social disadvantage rarely stretch far enough into the past to address the historic injustices committed against Aboriginal peoples in settler colonial contexts. Notions of distributive justice (Fleischacker, 2004) have been largely insensitive to the imposition of settler sovereignty and the extinguishment of customary rights to land and natural resources. We confront an additional layer of policy complexity when the core issues at stake lie precisely at the intersections of Indigenous spirituality and the management of natural resources.

## Postsecular repentance?

The postsecular experiment in political philosophy can be interpreted as a self-critical move on the part of liberal theorists who acknowledge that some recent versions of secular politics have had the effect of limiting freedom of religion, with unintended consequences. Habermas suggests that there is room for repentance in political practice, and he proposes a mutual engagement in public discourse within which neither religious nor secular parties remains quite what they were:

> [A] secularist attitude does not suffice for the expected cooperation with fellow citizens who are religious. This cognitive act of adaptation needs to be distinguished from the political virtue of mere tolerance. What is at stake is not some respectful feel for the possible existential significance of religion for some other person. What we must also expect of the secular

citizens is moreover a self-reflective transcending of a secularist self-understanding of modernity. (Habermas, 2006, p 15)

One of the problems with this laudable-sounding proposal, however, is that it seems to assume a modernist conception of 'religion' that is readily separable from a 'secular' mindset (cf King, 1999; Nongbri, 2013; Harrison, 2015). The idea that religion inhabits a discrete world of experience, separate from politics, economics and the environment, is one of the assumptions that needs further analysis. Even if this conceptual assumption is workable enough for European cultures (although even in that context a number of qualifications would be needed), it is manifestly unworkable in relation to Indigenous cultures. Aboriginal and Torres Strait Islander people in Australia regularly express their frustrations, for example, with the separate legislative regimes in Australia that govern land, natural resources, cultural heritage, and so on, all of which are integrated within traditional spirituality and governance. Our current legal system exemplifies the fragmentation and specialisation of the modern life world, and the invention of a special category called 'religion' is simply one illustration of the incommensurability between traditional Indigenous law and modern democratic arrangements. In short, 'modern' and 'pre-modern' assumptions exist simultaneously in postmodern Australia, and many of our political clashes reflect the contradictions that arise when settler colonial states attempt to recognise the enduring legal and social realities of Indigenous polities (see IPO, 2012).

Habermas rightly points out that the pursuit of reparations for past injustices towards Indigenous peoples can become embroiled in legal contradictions in part because democratic law can be 'insensitive to episodes that predate the legal system' (Habermas, 2008, pp 304-5). In the Australian context, we can think, for example, of such insensitivity even in the *Mabo* decision of the High Court in 1992, which resolved that the assertion of British sovereignty was non-judiciable (Keon-Cohen, 2011, p 59). Nevertheless, compensation for the extinguishment of native title could be available from 1975, the year that the Racial Discrimination Act became law. In short, the Court acknowledged the existence of native title at the establishment of the various Australian colonies, but decided that dispossession before 1975 could not be litigated in native title claims. We have thereby entrenched a structural racism within the legal history of Australia (Strelein, 2006, pp 20-3; cf Watson, 2011, pp 532-5). While a number of state governments – the successors to the separate colonial governments – had previously provided limited 'land rights' to Aboriginal groups, it was not until the *Mabo* case of 1992 that federal law recognised a fundamental problem in the way that land had been acquired at the assertion of British sovereignty.

Among the very few rights afforded by the Australian Constitution of 1901, Section 51 provided compensation on 'just terms' for the compulsory acquisition of land, but this provision was deemed inapplicable on the grounds that, under traditional law and custom, Aboriginal people did not hold land as a recognisable property right. Compensation for extinguishment of native title was therefore seen not as a remedy for compulsory acquisition of land, but rather as a remedy for the loss of a bundle of rights to exercise traditional activities like hunting, fishing and gathering natural resources under Indigenous law and custom (Pearson, 2004).

## Re-thinking rights

If reparations are to find their way into new political proposals, then any such proposals would require an account of corporate, intergenerational and cultural rights. The UN Declaration on the Rights of Indigenous Peoples presents a significant challenge for liberal traditions within which rights are supposed to be distributed across citizens equally, ideally on an individual rather than corporate basis. Some of the presumptions of liberal theory were illustrated by a public outcry at the time of the discovery of native title in Australia, when, for example, Senator Nick Minchin could claim that native title would become 'a vehicle for creating a lot of damage to the reconciliation process itself' since 'Aboriginal people have these special rights that other Australians don't have' (Brough, 1996, p 34; cf O'Connor, 1998, p 501). Minchin captured a popular sentiment in his political posturing, and this might be easily dismissed in some respects, but Habermas' comments on the limitations of legal systems in settler colonial states reflect deeper conceptual problems.

In his earlier work, Habermas attempted to distinguish, on the one hand, between universalisable 'norms' of public justice, and on the other, the narrower 'values' shaped by particular cultural or religious identities. In effect, 'values' were moved out of the sphere of public discourse and housed in the more sectarian contexts of culture and identity. Universalisable norms, according to the early Habermas,

> ... require a break with all of the unquestioned truths of an established, concrete ethical life, in addition to distancing oneself from the contexts of life with which one's identity is inextricably interwoven. (Habermas, 1990, p 12)

This procedural break with tradition and identity was recommended, in part, as an antidote to the excesses of ethnic nationalism, and in the German context this makes self-evidently good sense. Indeed, beyond any of the particularities of European expressions of nationalism, there are clear reasons why procedural limitations might well be placed on a dominant ethnicity within well-functioning democracies. Yet, when these procedural rules are translated into settler colonial contexts, and considered through the lens of subaltern groups, it becomes clear they do not simply limit the power of dominant ethnicities. It would seem that Indigenous people could only participate in the political process to the extent that they renounce the traditions and particularities that make them Indigenous. To put this point more broadly, the universalising assumptions of Habermas' 'ideal speech situation' seem to imply that cultural and religious identities as such are not sufficiently rational for the purposes of public dialogue (cf Stout, 2003, p 81).

Accordingly, a key question now arising for public policy in Australia – especially since the advent of the UN Declaration on the Rights of Indigenous Peoples (2007) – is how the human rights tradition can be expanded to embody collective rights. Habermas himself has begun this task in a more general way by exploring the conditions under which multiple cultures can flourish through differentiated concepts of citizenship, which may be constituted democratically within a nation-state (see, for example, Habermas, 2008, pp 271-311). While he does not attribute rights to cultures as such, he does contemplate the ways in which the bearers of a culture might enjoy collective or corporate rights within a multicultural democracy.

As we have seen, however, he acknowledges that there are special problems when the culture at issue is Indigenous and it is maintained within settler colonial states like the USA, Australia and New Zealand. For the purposes of our present discussion, therefore, it is necessary to begin with an analogy between cultural and religious traditions, bearing in mind that they present similar kinds of problems of access into public discourse. A conceptual linkage between culture and religion is no longer self-evident, but in the case of traditional Indigenous polities, it is quite clear that religion, spiritualty and culture are all interwoven. It may be illuminating as a heuristic exercise to redact one of the arguments in Habermas' essay 'Religion in the public sphere' by glossing the term 'religious' with the word 'Indigenous':

> The liberal state has an interest in unleashing religious [or Indigenous] voices in the political public sphere, and in the political participation of religious organizations as well. It must not discourage religious persons and communities [or Indigenous persons and communities] from also expressing themselves politically as such, for it cannot know whether secular society would not otherwise cut itself off from key resources for the creation of meaning and identity. Secular citizens or those of other religious persuasions can under certain circumstances learn something from religious contributions; this is, for example, the case if they recognize in the normative truth content of a religious utterance hidden intuitions of their own. (Habermas, 2006, p 10)

Habermas suggests that a religious tradition that appears to be merely sectarian could in fact have something to share more widely when it is translated into accessible language. He freely acknowledges that this has happened in liberal societies since the Enlightenment, but a measure of discomfort arises when it is suggested that something similar might apply to Indigenous culture/religion.

Habermas acknowledges that the human rights tradition was in part inspired by the claim in Genesis 1 that humans are made in the 'image of God', a claim that has been secularised with redemptive effects when translated into public discourse beyond the limits of Jewish and Christian scripture: 'The translation of the human likeness to God [*Gottesebenbildlichkeit*] into the equal dignity of all humans, a dignity to be respected unconditionally, is such a saving translation' (Habermas, 2004, p 346; cf Waldron, 2010). He acknowledges in this connection the enormous contribution of Martin Luther King Jr, who could translate the specific cadences of black Baptist preaching into a generalised advocacy of civil rights (Habermas, 2008, p 124; cf Stout, 2003, p 81). Comparable arguments for translating other religious traditions into human rights discourse have been advanced by numerous authors (for example, Küng and Moltmann, 1990; Runzo et al, 2003).

The civil rights movements in the USA, South Africa and Australia illustrate a remarkable irony in the way that a religious tradition can be reconfigured. Colonial Christianity had injected virulent strains of racism into each of these contexts, yet it was the very same Christian tradition that joined cause with Martin Luther King, Bishop Tutu and the Christian Aboriginal leader in Australia, Douglas Nicholls, to address the historic injustices of the colonial past (Brett, 2016, pp 1-3). These cases illustrate the memorable definition of a tradition proposed by Alasdair MacIntyre: 'a living tradition is an historically extended, socially embodied argument, and an argument precisely in part about the goods which constitute that tradition' (1981, p 207). The catalogue of complaints that can be brought against colonial Christianity is so impressive one might wonder why it is still the majority religion of many countries in Africa, Latin America and Oceania (Sanneh, 2003). Nevertheless, this short list of transformative leaders – Martin Luther King, Bishop Tutu, Douglas Nicholls – illustrates the possibility that

Christian tradition can be reformulated in dialogue with Indigenous traditions (Bevis, 2016).

## Concepts of justice and religious traditions

The historic injustices of colonialism could still be characterised in the 1960s as belonging to 'the great Australian silence' (Stanner, 2009, pp 182-93), but from the 1970s onwards there have been a flurry of Indigenous policies arising from distributive notions of social justice. Nevertheless, we have barely begun to grasp the kind of recognition that might undermine the legitimacy of settler sovereignty (cf Fraser and Honneth, 2003). Although each concept of justice may have its own validity in particular contexts of application, in settler colonial contexts we need to develop practices of restorative justice that pay attention to the tensions and contradictions that may be generated by distributive and utilitarian claims. More importantly, I would also argue that explicit engagement with a variety of religious traditions will play an important part in any substantial practice of reconciliation. This engagement might well be characterised as postsecular, not because it entails a return to pre-modern imaginaries, but because it will enable new depths of public discourse that embrace the complexity of mutable religious traditions.

There are a number of restorative strategies that have demonstrated their value in postcolonial contexts, and in *Just and unjust peace: A political ethic of reconciliation* (2012), Daniel Philpott proposed the combined practices of acknowledgment, reparations, punishment, apology, forgiveness and the establishment of just institutions (cf Langton, 2006; Vorster, 2006). Taken together, these practices constitute a political ethic of reconciliation founded on restorative justice rather than distributive or utilitarian norms. Philpott also shows how these practices can be underpinned by a variety of religious traditions, especially Jewish, Christian and Islamic traditions. My recent book *Political trauma and healing* develops Philpott's model, in particular re-reading biblical traditions in ways that make space for Indigenous spiritualities. Beyond the familiar suggestion that human rights arguments can arise from the unity of all human beings asserted in Genesis 1, a broader creation theology can also underpin the rights of non-human animals in ways that build links with Indigenous spiritualities (Brett, 2016).

For those who are inclined to see religion and secularity as a zero-sum game, an objection will, of course, spring immediately to mind: 'religious' warrants would only be relevant for those portions of Australian society who continue to find such arguments in some sense edifying, and public debates are not an appropriate context for citing religious arguments, even if their purpose is to undermine the ethnocentrism of the dominant culture or historic injustices (cf Rawls, 1997). I want to make two main points in response to this kind of secular objection.

First, if census figures may be taken as indicative, more than half of the Australian population might find specifically Christian arguments relevant for thinking about the task of reconciliation. It is well known that Australian sensitivities lie worlds away from the extravagant expressions of religiosity that may still be found in North American politics, but the residual commitments to Christian identity in Australian census figures point to a broader spiritual legacy beyond commitment to any particular church tradition. No doubt many of the individuals behind these statistics are travelling 'with light metaphysical baggage', to borrow a phrase from Habermas (2008, pp 262, 309), but that lightness of being would not exclude the possibility that arguments for restorative justice can be drawn from religious sources. Indeed, the attempt to promote postsecular discourse in Habermas' recent writing points precisely to the possibility of shaping public conversation in dialogue with neglected 'religious' sources that may yet have relevance beyond the narrow confines where they were consigned by modernity. In particular, the idea of religious liberty might yet yield affirmations of Indigenous rights that were historically denied. For example, I argue below that the affirmation of natural rights in the 1830s might well be rejuvenated today within a variety of Christian constituencies, even given the significant cultural shifts between the 19th and 21st centuries.

Second, it is not necessary to create a single theory of Indigenous rights to underpin public policy, but only to clarify the motivations that would allow a variety of different groups – tradition by tradition – to reach a sufficient measure of agreement. On this point, I wholeheartedly agree with the pragmatic approach taken by Amartya Sen in his work on *The idea of justice* (2009), namely, that human rights instruments can travel with light metaphysical baggage if an overlapping consensus in public discourse actually helps to make the world a little less unjust than it currently is.

In that pragmatic spirit, a new kind of inter-religious engagement in the making of Indigenous policy could pay attention to a broad range of religious traditions while giving prominence to the practical applications of Aboriginal spirituality in the major areas of public policy: law, education, community services, management of natural resources and the development of culturally appropriate economic strategies (see, for example, Altman, 2010). A version of this argument has already been proposed from a Muslim perspective by the Indigenous lawyer Asmi Wood (2015).

In the current cultural climate, it would also be important to range more widely into multiple understandings of spirituality beyond the narrowly conceived notions of religion. For example, a national enquiry into the removal of Aboriginal and Islander children from their families (*Bringing them home*, Human Rights and Equal Opportunity Commission, 1997) proposed a broad range of initiatives for healing the intergenerational trauma, including a broader conception of therapeutic healing that includes spiritual and cultural renewal. Writing in response to the *Bringing them home* report, the Aboriginal and Torres Strait Islander Social Justice Commissioner, Tom Calma, affirmed that 'Spirituality is largely outside the dominant paradigm of policy makers and funding bodies in Australia, yet it is an intrinsic part of healing' (Aboriginal and Torres Strait Islander Social Justice Commissioner, 2009, p 152; cf Philips, 2007; Cooper, 2011).

My argument proposes that democratic discourse is not best served by a thinning of public norms in search of a unified public culture, but rather by a thickening of dialogue between religious and non-religious traditions in the pursuit of more inclusive democracies. The clarity of public policy is not well served by the exclusion of religious discourse; on the contrary, it is enhanced by its disciplined inclusion.

To that end, it will be helpful to re-examine some of the classic religious defences of multicultural and multireligious societies, especially where we find clear acknowledgment of Indigenous rights. The example set by Roger Williams in the settlement of Rhode Island is worthy of consideration, as Martha Nussbaum (2008) has shown in her book, *Liberty of conscience*. But she still tends to follow the tradition of reading the Rhode Island settlement as a remarkable phenomenon in American legal history, rather than locating that story within the innovative political theology of the Baptists. For Williams that theology implied a wholesale rejection of the Puritan version of the doctrine of discovery (Eberle, 2005; Freeman, 2007). The affirmation of the liberty of conscience in this Baptist tradition arguably yielded a much more radical embrace of Indigenous rights than was achieved in other defences of Indigenous rights in Protestant circles, notably in the framework of international law provided by Hugo Grotius (cf Wilson, 2008, pp 467-512).

In the rapidly expanding Anglo colonies of the 1830s, it was still possible to appreciate the 'natural rights' of Indigenous peoples, and this is well illustrated by the advocacy of the Aborigines Protection Society and by the initiatives proposed by the Colonial Office in London at the time (Knaplund, 1953; Brennan, 2010). In the foundation of the colony of South Australia, for example, a new legal requirement was imposed requiring evidence of treaties with Aboriginal people before their land was ceded to the Crown. The requirement lasted barely half a decade, and tragically bore no fruit before it was overwhelmed by the weight of economic interests in subsequent decades (Brett, 2014).

The discourse of natural rights had fallen into disrepute by the end of the 19th century due, in part, to the influence of Jeremy Bentham's brand of utilitarianism. Their rebirth as 'human rights' were effected mainly through the trauma of the Second World War and the creation of the United Nations (UN), and it must be acknowledged that even in 1948 the Christian churches played a significant role behind the scenes of the UN Declaration of Human Rights (Nurser, 2005). There was still a long road to travel to the UN Declaration on the Rights of Indigenous Peoples (2007), and in this renewal of Indigenous rights some religious actors are also playing their part, although a lot of work remains to be done (Heinrichs, 2016).

In recent years, some senior Christian leaders in Australia have even shown a lack of capacity to deal with the more general discourse of human rights. Many church groups opposed the introduction of a federal Charter of Rights let alone the kind of constitutional changes that would be necessary to entrench Indigenous rights more deeply into our legal tradition (Calma and Gershevitch, 2009). Such recent examples of shallow disregard for human rights instruments point to the peculiarity of the Australian context, but in my view, they should provoke a stronger determination to re-engage with the historic Christian defences of the natural rights of Indigenous peoples. The research agenda of scholars in Religious Studies, Politics, History and Law should be enriched to include the variety of possible approaches to the UN Declaration on the Rights of Indigenous Peoples from the point of view of each of the major religious traditions represented in Australian society.

## Conclusion

The time is ripe for prising open the trinity of state, sovereignty and jurisdiction, and for embracing the thickly textured polities that exist in the social space between the individual and the state – precisely when such polities self-identify as religious, or, as in the case of Indigenous people, when the very category of religion amounts to a problematic imposition on lived experience. For liberal theorists like Habermas, a renewed engagement with complex webs of spirituality might be styled as 'postsecular', but it would also be possible to see this engagement as a reconsideration of some models of secularity advocated in 17th- and 18th-century Europe. Ironically, this would also perhaps open up new avenues of engagement with the secular practices of government in the Asia-Pacific region (Bouma et al, 2010), which are less allergic to religious traditions.

## References

Aboriginal and Torres Strait Islander Social Justice Commissioner (2009) *Social justice report 2008*, Sydney, NSW: Australian Human Rights Commission.

Altman, J. (2010) 'What future for remote Indigenous Australia? Economic hybridity and neo-liberal turn', in J. Altman and M. Hinkson (eds) *Culture crisis: Anthropology and politics in Aboriginal Australia*, Sydney, NSW: University of New South Wales Press, pp 259-80.

Bevis, S. (2016) 'New songs and old songlines: Aboriginal Christianity and post-mission Australia', in J.L. Cox and A. Possamai (eds) *Religion and non-religion among Australian Aboriginal Peoples*, Abingdon: Routledge, pp 129-56.

Bouma, G., Ling, R. and Pratt, D.P. (eds) (2010) *Religious diversity in Southeast Asia and the Pacific: National case studies*, Dordrecht: Springer.

Brennan, S. (2010) 'The disregard for legal protections of Aboriginal land rights in early South Australia', in S. Berg (ed) *Coming to terms: Aboriginal title in South Australia*, Kent Town, SA: Wakefield Press, pp 90-121.

Brett, M.G. (2014) 'Law and sovereignty in Australian national narratives', in M.G. Brett and J. Havea (eds) *Colonial contexts and postcolonial theologies: Storyweaving in the Asia-Pacific*, New York: Palgrave Macmillan, pp 161-77.

Brett, M.G. (2016) *Political trauma and healing: Biblical ethics for a postcolonial world*, Grand Rapids, MI: Eerdmans.

Brough, J. (1996) 'Chorus of criticism for Howard's negotiator', *Sydney Morning Herald*, 1 June, p 34.

Calma, T. and Gershevitch, C. (2009) *Freedom of religion and belief in a multicultural democracy: An inherent contradiction or an achievable human right?*, Australian Human Rights Commission (www.humanrights.gov.au/about-australian-human-rights-commission).

Cooper, D. (2011) *Closing the gap in cultural understanding: Social determinants of health and indigenous policy in Australia*, Darwin, NT: Aboriginal Medical Services Alliance NT.

Eberle, E.J. (2005) 'Roger Williams on liberty of conscience', *Roger Williams University Law Review*, vol 10, no 2, pp 289-323.

Fleischacker, S. (2004) *A short history of distributive justice*, Cambridge, MA: Harvard University Press.

Fraser, N. and Honneth, A. (2003) *Redistribution or recognition? A political philosophical exchange* (translated by J. Golb and C. Wilke), London: Verso.

Freeman, C.W. (2007) 'Roger Williams, American democracy, and the Baptists', *Perspectives in Religious Studies*, vol 34, no 3, pp 267-86.

Habermas, J. (2004) 'On the relation between the secular liberal state and religion', in E. Mendieta (ed) *The Frankfurt School on Religion*, New York: Routledge, pp 337-46.

Habermas, J. (2006) 'Religion in the public sphere', *European Journal of Philosophy*, vol 14, no 1, pp 1-25.

Habermas, J. (2008) *Between naturalism and religion* (translated by C. Cronin), Cambridge: Polity Press.

Habermas, J. (2009) *Justification and application* (translated by C. Lenhardt), Oxford: Polity Press.

Harrison, P. (2015) *The territories of science and religion*, Chicago, IL: University of Chicago Press.

Heinrichs, S. (ed) (2016) *Wrongs to rights: How churches can engage the United Nations Declaration on the Rights of Indigenous Peoples*, Winnipeg, MB: Mennonite Church Canada.

Human Rights and Equal Opportunity Commission (1997) *Bringing them home: Report of the National Inquiry into the Separation of Aboriginal and Torres Strait Islander Children from Their Families*, Sydney, NSW: HREOC.

IPO (Indigenous Peoples Organisations) (2012) *Report of the IPO Network of Australia to the United Nations Permanent Forum on Indigenous Issues, Eleventh Session – New York, 7-18 May, 2012. The Doctrine of discovery: Its enduring impact on Indigenous Peoples of Australia and the right to redress (Articles 28 and 37 of the United Nations Declaration on the Rights of Indigenous Peoples)*.

Keon-Cohen, B. (2011) *Mabo in the courts: Islander tradition to Native Title*, Melbourne, VIC: Chancery Bold.

King, R. (1999) *Orientalism and religion: Postcolonial theory, India and 'the mystic East'*, London: Routledge.

Knaplund, P. (1953) *James Stephen and the British colonial system, 1813-1847*, Madison, WI: University of Wisconsin Press.

Küng, H. and Moltmann, J. (eds) (1990) *The ethics of world religions and human rights*, London: SCM.

Langton, M., Mazel, O., Palmer, L., Shain, K. and Tehan, M. (eds) (2006) *Settling with Indigenous people: Modern treaty and agreement-making*, Sydney, NSW: The Federation Press.

MacIntyre, A. (1981) *After virtue*, Notre Dame, Paris: University of Notre Dame Press.

Nongbri, B. (2013) *Before religion: The history of a modern concept*, New Haven, CT: Yale University Press.

Nurser, J. (2005) *For all peoples and all nations: Christian churches and human rights*, Washington, DC: Georgetown University Press.

Nussbaum, M.C. (2008) *Liberty of conscience: In defense of American's tradition of religious equality*, New York: Basic Books.

O'Connor, P. (1998) 'Indigenous policy, Native Title and the rule of law', *Agenda*, vol 5, no 4, pp 501-8.

Pearson, N. (2004) 'Land is capable of ownership', in M. Langton, M. Tehan, L. Palmer and K. Shain (eds) *Honour among nations? Treaties and agreements with Indigenous people*, Melbourne, VIC: Melbourne University Press, pp 83-100.

Philips, G. (2007) 'Healing and public policy', in J. Altman and M. Hinkson (eds) *Coercive reconciliation: Stabilise, normalise, exit Aboriginal Australia*, Melbourne, VIC: Arena, pp 141-50.

Philpott, D. (2012) *Just and unjust peace: An ethic of political reconciliation*, Oxford: Oxford University Press.

Rawls, J. (1997) 'The idea of public reason revisited', *The University of Chicago Law Review*, vol 64, no 3, pp 765-807.

Runzo, J., Martin, N.M., and Sharma, A. (eds) (2003) *Human rights and responsibilities in the world religions*, Oxford: Oneworld.

Sanneh, L. (2003) *Whose religion is Christianity? The gospel beyond the west*, Grand Rapids, MI: Eerdmans.

Sen, A. (2009) *The idea of justice*, London: Allen Lane.

Stanner, W.E.G. (2009) *The Dreaming and other essays*, Melbourne, VIC: Black Inc.

Stout, J. (2003) *Democracy and tradition*, Princeton, NJ: Princeton University Press.

Strelein, L. (2006) *Compromised jurisprudence: Native title cases since Mabo*, Canberra, ACT: Aboriginal Studies Press.

Vorster, J.M. (2006) 'The ethics of land restitution', *Journal of Religious Ethics*, vol 34, no 4, pp 685-707.

Waldron, J. (2010) 'The image of God: Rights, reason and order', in J. Witte Jr and F.S. Alexander (eds) *Christianity and human rights: An introduction*, Cambridge: Cambridge University Press, pp 216-35.

Watson, B.A. (2011) 'John Marshall and Indian land rights: A historical rejoinder to the claim of "Universal Recognition" of the Doctrine of Discovery', *Seton Hall Law Review*, vol 36, no 2, pp 481-549.

Wilson, E. (2008) *Savage Republic: De Indis of Hugo Grotius, republicanism and Dutch hegemony within the early modern world system, c 1600-1619*, Leiden: Brill.

Wood, A. (2015) 'Indigenous spiritual light: Reconsidering the negative stereotypes on indigenous spirituality', in D. Iner and S. Yucel (eds) *Muslim identity formation in religiously diverse societies*, Newcastle upon Tyne: Cambridge Scholars Publishing, pp 266-89.

# EIGHT

# Re-imagining the place of religion in the workplace: The example of Australian social work

Beth R. Crisp

## Introduction

In an Australian novel set in the late 1920s on a cruise, the heroine contemplates the Sunday options available to passengers and crew:

> Attending various forms of divine service, perhaps (Catholic in the second class chapel, sung Eucharist in the first class chapel, Buddhists and pagans presumably to make their own arrangements)? (Greenwood, 2005, p 141)

Indeed class differentiation of religion has been a feature of Australian society since European settlement commenced in 1788 as a penal colony. Among the early settlers, the military and free settlers tended to be Anglican or Presbyterian, but convicts and former convicts were disproportionately Catholic. Assumptions that Protestantism was essentially the religion of the ruling class held through much of the

20th century, with other scenarios not even entertained in the public imagination (Dempsey, 1983).

Similarly, within the profession of social work, it is not uncommon to hear matters of religion discussed with a certain assuredness that no other possibility is imaginable. Over the last two decades there has been a growing interest in the role of religion and spirituality in social work practice internationally, including in countries such as Australia, places where for much of the 20th century social work sought to distance itself from its religious roots. However, while there is now much wider recognition that religion and spirituality can make a very positive contribution to wellbeing for individuals and communities, the professional imagination as to what this might involve has frequently been confined to particular situations, stages of life or fields of practice (Crisp, 2017).

## Provision of welfare services by religious organisations

Differentiation by class differentiation on the basis of religion has been accompanied in Australia by a segmentation of welfare services by religion (Hughes, 1998). Unlike in some countries where the emergence of the welfare state saw religious groups hand over much of their welfare provision to the state (Prochaska, 2006), religious organisations remain major providers of health and welfare services to the Australian community, albeit much of it on contract to government departments and paid for by taxpayers (Crisp, 2014). Almost all of the 25 largest Australian charities are associated with organisations where religious beliefs underpin their existence (Lake, 2013). Moreover, Bishop Michael Challen's (1996, p 26) comment some 20 years ago as Director of the Anglican welfare agency the Brotherhood of St Laurence when he said 'The people of Australia expect the Churches to be active in the care of people, whether they are members or not' is still likely to find considerable agreement within the Australian community. Nevertheless, various inquiries, including the Royal Commission into Institutional Responses to Child Sexual Abuse, have certainly brought out more public questioning as to the capacity of some religious organisations to provide appropriate services to vulnerable members of the Australian community (Healy, 2015; McPhillips, 2017). This comes after the recognition that in past decades church organisations were involved in the removal of Indigenous children from their families and communities, in what has become known as the 'Stolen Generation', forcing unmarried mothers to relinquish babies for adoption, and the mistreatment of child migrants sent from residential care providers in the UK (Crisp, 2014; Healy, 2015). The following statement, originally made about the place of women in the Church of Sweden, might readily apply to responses in the Australian community to religious welfare organisations where cultures of abuse and/or neglect have flourished:

> Questions posed include how to deal with the shifts in perceptions of authority which challenge old, hierarchical patterns of governance. They also include how to deal with the fact that churches, in spite of their claim to be transmitters of justification and forgiveness, regularly fail in their practice to be just communities of equal and responsible citizens. (Edgardh Beckman, 2001, p 12)

In the 2017 survey of Australian voters about marriage equality, many religious leaders and many religious congregations publicly supported the proposal that marriage should be available to both heterosexual and same-sex couples. However, my own experience in casual conversations was that strangers would often be surprised to find people of faith who supported marriage equality. However, this is not surprising as religious voices on social issues that gain the most media coverage in many communities tend to be those that are out of step with wider society values (Landau, 2012), such as promoting prohibitionism – anti-drinking, anti-gambling, anti-sex, anti-abortion etc – even when such views are not necessarily held universally by members of a religious group (Dixon, 2014). This may tell us more about media outlets and their priorities than it does about religious beliefs in the community:

... it is sex, violence, exoticism, personalities, power plays, extremism and menacing commitment that sells website space as well as newspapers. This tells you as much about certain styles of media and reporting regimes as it does about different types of religion or belief. (Barrow, 2012, p 180)

## Religion and social work

It is perhaps not surprising that such understandings of religion do not fit well with a profession that champions notions such as 'liberation of people' and 'social justice'. However, arguably there is a high degree of synergy between many religious teachings and the latest definition of social work approved in 2014 by the International Federation of Social Workers (IFSW) and the International Association of Schools of Social Work (IASSW):

Social work is a practice-based profession and an academic discipline that promotes social change and development, social cohesion, and the empowerment and liberation of people. Principles of social justice, human rights, collective responsibility and respect for diversities are central to social work. Underpinned by theories of social work, social sciences, humanities and indigenous knowledge, social work engages people and structures to address life challenges and enhance wellbeing. (IFSW and IASSW, 2014)

If the Australian community has a somewhat complicated view on the place of religious organisations providing welfare services, so, too, do Australian social workers. Every year as I review prospective social work students, there are some applicants who make explicit their desire to work in a field that they perceive as enabling them to live out their own religious beliefs. Information provided by other applicants suggests that for some this desire is implicit (see also Crisp, 2014). In my own case, when I applied to study social work, one university required applicants to attend an interview. Despite having completed a Bachelor of Arts (Honours) degree in Political Science and working in a graduate position in a government department, almost all the questions were based on the fact that I had commenced a Theology degree and seemed to be about ensuring I was not a religious fanatic. Although I must have passed whatever test I was being subjected to, I took up an offer from another university where having religious beliefs was not so apparently problematic. It was only later that I was to learn that religious social workers/social work students are often deemed to be conservative, judgmental or oppressive (Anderson-Nathe et al, 2013).

## Religion and social work education

The only survey of religious beliefs among Australia's social work educators was conducted in 1999, more than a decade after I commenced my social work education. This found two-thirds claiming no religious affiliation compared to less than one-third of the wider Australian population at the time (Lindsay, 2002). Although not necessarily representative of the wider profession, social work educators are influential in that they are entrusted with the nurture of future generations of practitioners. Consequently, there are generations of social work graduates whose only memory of matters associated with religion being discussed was an exotic feature of a case study or as something problematic (Lindsay, 2002; Crisp, 2015). Students' experiences as part of their compulsory supervised placements will often reinforce the ideas that social workers do not consider religion as a relevant in people's lives (Askeland and Døhlie, 2015). Consequently, students can graduate without the idea that religious beliefs or membership of a religious community may be potentially rich resources for some individuals and communities ever being raised (Furness and Gilligan, 2010).

Looking back, the lack of discussion about matters religious in late 20th-century social work education in Australia reflects the desire of social workers in many countries to distance their profession from its religious roots due to the perception that religion and professionalism are antithetical (Crisp, 2017). As one of very few health professions not covered by the registration provisions of the Australian Health Practitioner Regulation Agency (AHPRA), professional recognition remains important, but the arguments have moved on and are no longer about differentiating social work from any religious antecedents (Healy, 2015).

The *Global standards for social work education and training* (IFSW and IASSW, 2004) that were ratified in 2004 noted the need to respect religious beliefs and to recognise the potential for religion to be a resource. In terms of 'Standards with regard to social work students', religion was explicitly listed in a list of characteristics for which there should be 'non-discrimination against any student on the basis of …' (IFSW and IASSW, 2004, p 9).

## Religion and social work practice

In 2010, the Australian Association of Social Workers (AASW) revised its *Code of ethics* with more explicit recognition of the need to respect a diversity of religious beliefs and practices:

> Social workers will recognise, acknowledge and remain sensitive to and respectful of the religious and spiritual world views of individuals, groups, communities and social networks, and the operations and missions of faith and spiritually-based organisations. (AASW, 2010, p 18)

If there are clauses that social workers have not read or not comprehended in the *Code of ethics*, those pertaining to religion would arguably be at the top of the list. Australian social workers are often ambivalent, if not antagonistic, towards religion, as reflected in the AASW's recent statement that religion is one of the 'discriminatory structures and practices, in Australia, based on dominant cultural norms' (AASW, 2017 p 18).

Recently I was listening to a woman tell me about her experience as an inpatient in the state of Victoria's mental health system. The antagonism towards people of faith, both patients and the hospital chaplains, was overt, and she considered the social workers were among the worst offenders. In response to her answer that her previous occupation had been Minister of Religion was written a file note 'major delusions of grandeur'. In my experience, the irony is that most ministers of religion I know are the first to admit they are not God, and this woman has spent much of her working life breaking down such expectations of others that she was God. Furthermore, it seems that despite many of the mainline Protestant churches in Australia having ordained women as ministers for a number of decades, this possibility was not acknowledged.

While its predecessor had acknowledged requirements to prevent discrimination on the basis of religion, the need for social workers to remain aware of conflicts of interest on the basis of religion and the need to be aware of their own religious values (AASW, 1999), the current *Code of ethics* for Australian social workers (AASW, 2010) for the first time recognised the right for social workers to have their own religious or spiritual beliefs respected within the workplace. The *Code of ethics* also now acknowledges that tackling social problems may require social workers to forge partnerships with religious organisations:

> Social workers will engage in respectful collaborative relationships with their colleagues from different ethnic, cultural, religious and other backgrounds and identities. These working relationships may at times need to extend to … the development and provision of culturally safe and appropriate services. (AASW, 2010, p 18)

## Working in partnership with religious organisations

Despite the reach of religious organisations into their communities often extending far beyond that of initiatives of other service providers (Strickland et al, 1998), the potential of such partnerships often fails to be recognised, particularly around issues where religious organisations are perceived as having a poor track record, such as gender-based violence (Dyer, 2010). As people of influence in their communities, religious leaders can contribute to violence prevention efforts (Colpitts, 2014). As Australian social work academic Sarah Wendt has suggested,

> If social institutions, such as the church, become more aware of the dynamics and complexities of domestic violence and understand how power and control operate in violent situations, particular discourses that shape experiences of domestic violence can be challenged and resisted. (2008, p 152)

However, religious organisations may need outside assistance to identify how they can contribute to efforts to prevent domestic violence occurring, and appropriately respond when it does occur. To this end, in Victoria the Victorian Health Promotion Foundation has contributed to a number of projects that have involved partnerships with faith communities or religious networks (City of Casey, 2009; Holmes, 2012; Boddé, 2013). Apart from engaging with pivotal individuals who can ensure the issues are placed on the organisational agenda, those initiatives that have been most promising are those that have engaged with the religious beliefs and language of the target group. For example, one local project reported that:

> Questions of formal and informal leadership within faith communities, of the relation between faith and culture, of the religious use and understanding of language around gender, and of the complex diversity of the faith setting posed challenges to a clear sense of project direction and purpose. (Holmes, 2012, p 16)

Catholic author David Ranson of the Broken Bay Diocese has very eloquently written of the need for a bilingualism when working with religious organisations:

> How does a ... become "bi-lingual", that is, both theologically literate and professionally literate, such that the same reality can

be expressed in two different ways without compromise to either theological or professional discourse?

What is the right balance between these two "languages"? Which "language" is best to be used? When? How? With whom? And by whom? (Ranson, 2008, p 91)

Arguably seeking to understand the language and culture is something any Social Work 101 student is taught, but too often health and welfare professionals seek to impose their own language and ways of doing things in partnership arrangements. Furthermore, perceptions from professionals involved in violence prevention that religious communities are not open to addressing issues of gender-based violence may actually have hindered opportunities to engage with religious communities around issues these issues (City of Casey, 2009).

## The need for religious literacy

Just as religious organisations may be lacking in knowledge of how to best respond to specific social problems, Australian social workers often lack the degree of religious literacy that may be required to work effectively with individuals, groups or organisations for whom their religious beliefs or practices are integral to their sense of identity, such as the earlier example of the woman in a mental health facility. A lack of religious literacy also manifests itself in using 'religion' as a euphemism for culture or ethnicity or vice versa.

If we accept the fact that religion is important to the majority of people living on this planet, and if the work of social workers is about working with people, then arguably social workers require a degree of religious literacy in order to practice their profession. However, Australian social workers typically have very limited, if any, knowledge of the key beliefs and practices of religions beyond those they identify or affiliate with, and sometimes even of the religions they nominally identify with. Moreover, with steadily declining participation rates in religious worship over recent decades, unless social workers have a personal interest, their knowledge of religion(s) tends to be extremely limited (Crisp, 2015).

A seemingly obvious way of addressing religious illiteracy would be that professional social work education should incorporate learning about religion, perhaps the place of religion in the lives of individuals and societies, as well as key teachings and practices of major world religions. However, as any of my fellow heads of social work programmes in Australia's higher education institutions could tell you, the accreditation requirements for social work courses in Australia result in many important issues receiving minimal, if any, coverage if it is not mandated. As the profession already has various Royal Commissions lining up to say what social work students should be taught, the likelihood that students will receive any substantial learning about religion is unlikely. Furthermore, even if students have the opportunity to take electives from other parts of their university as part of their degree studies, many Australian universities do not have a religious studies programme from which they could select units of study to contribute to their Social Work degree (Boer, 2008). Conversely, elective options are only likely to be taken by students who already have some knowledge and interest in matters pertaining to religion.

## Conclusion

The discovery of religion by the social work profession is certainly not a panacea to a myriad of social problems. Indeed, religious teachings are frequently misused in welfare settings in ways that are abusive and show a lack of regard for individuals, families and communities. Consequently, like many sensitive topics, social workers should not force conversations about religion with service users. Conversely, and I suspect what happens more often, is that social workers need to be able to listen to what is said on matters religious and not change the topic to one they are more comfortable with (Crisp, 2010).

Finally, while there are certainly challenges and issues, there is a growing recognition among Australia's social workers that working holistically cannot exclude reference to religious beliefs and practices for those service users for whom this is important, although arguably

Australian social workers are more comfortable discussing spirituality than religion (Crisp, 2017). Imagining a role for religion in their professional lives will require a re-imagining as to what social work itself could be. While prudence is understandable and it is right that social workers should ensure that they don't place vulnerable service users at risk, ignoring the religious dimension of people's lives also has consequences. Re-imagining the place of religion in social work will not easily be realised, but not even entertaining this possibility might ultimately be even more problematic.

## References

AASW (Australian Association of Social Workers) (1999) *Code of ethics*, Canberra, ACT: AASW.

AASW (2010) *Code of ethics*, Canberra: AASW (www.aasw.asn.au/document/item/1201).

AASW (2017) *Australian Social Work Education and Accreditation Standards (ASWEAS) May 2017*, North Melbourne, VIC: AASW.

Anderson-Nathe, B., Gringer, C. and Wahab, S. (2013) 'Nurturing "critical hope" in teaching feminist social work research', *Journal of Social Work Education*, vol 49, no 2, pp 277-91.

Askeland, G.A. and Døhlie, E. (2015) 'Contextualizing international social work: Religion as a relevant factor', *International Social Work*, vol 58, no 2, pp 261-9.

Barrow, S. (2012) 'Religion and new media: Changing the story', in J. Mitchell and O. Gower (eds) *Religion and the news*, Farnham: Ashgate, pp 173-82.

Boddé, R. (2013) *Preventing violence against women: What works and what doesn't in Anglican communities*, Melbourne, VIC: Anglican Diocese of Melbourne (www.anglican.org.au/home/documents/news-and-media-releases/preventing%20violence%20against%20women%20%282013%29.pdf).

Boer, R. (2008) 'The new secularism', *Arena Journal*, no 29/30, pp 35-57.

Challen, M.B. (1996) 'The changing roles of church and state in Australian welfare provision', *Social Security Journal*, June, pp 26-31.

City of Casey (2009) 'Promoting peace in families model package', Narre Warren, VIC (www.casey.vic.gov.au/health-safety/health-promotion/family-violence-prevention).

Colpitts, E. (2014) 'Working with men to prevent and address violence against women: South African perspectives', Master of Arts thesis, Dalhousie University (http://dalspace.library.dal.ca/handle/10222/53993).

Crisp, B.R. (2010) *Spirituality and social work*, Farnham: Ashgate.

Crisp, B.R. (2014) *Social work and faith-based organizations*, London: Routledge.

Crisp, B.R. (2015) 'Religious literacy and social work: The view from Australia', in A. Dinham and M. Francis (eds) *Religious literacy: Enhancing understanding and cooperation*, Bristol: Policy Press, pp 207-26.

Crisp, B.R. (ed) (2017) *The Routledge handbook of religion, spirituality and social work*, London: Routledge.

Dempsey, K. (1983) *Conflict and decline: Ministers and laymen in an Australian country town*, North Ryde, NSW: Methuen.

Dixon, R. (2014) 'The changing face of the Catholic community in Australia: Challenges for Catholic social service organisations', in G. McMullen and J. Warhurst (eds) *Listening, learning and leading: The impact of catholic identity and mission*, Ballarat, VIC: Connor Court Publishing, pp 123-39.

Dyer, J. (2010) 'Challenging assumptions: Clergy perspectives and practices regarding intimate partner violence', *Journal of Religion and Spirituality in Social Work*, vol 29, no 1, pp 33-48.

Edgardh Beckman, N. (2001), 'Mrs Murphy's arising from the pew: Ecclesiological implications', *Ecumenical Review*, vol 5, no 1, pp 5-13.

Furness, S. and Gilligan, P. (2010) *Religion, belief and social work: Making a difference*, Bristol: Policy Press.

Greenwood, K. (2005) *Death by water*, Crows Nest, NSW: Allen & Unwin.

Healy, K. (2015) 2015 'Norma Parker address: being a self-regulating profession in the 21st century: Problems and prospects', *Australian Social Work*, vol 69, no 1, pp 1-10.

Holmes, S. (2012) *Northern Interfaith Respectful Relationships: Project report* (www.vichealth.vic.gov.au/~/media/ResourceCentre/PublicationsandResources/PVAW/Sharing%20the%20evidence_NIRR%202012.pdf?la=en).

Hughes, L. (1998) 'Catholics and the care of destitute children in late nineteenth century New South Wales', *Australian Social Work*, vol 51, no 1, pp 17-25.

IFSW (International Federation of Social Workers) and IASSW (International Association of Schools of Social Work) (2004) *Global standards for social work education and training* (http://cdn.ifsw.org/assets/ifsw_65044-3.pdf).

IFSW and IASSW (2014) 'Global definition of social work' (http://ifsw.org/get-involved/global-definition-of-social-work/).

Lake, M. (2013) *Faith in Action: Hammond Care*, Sydney, NSW: University of New South Wales Press.

Landau, C. (2012) 'What the media thinks about religion: A broadcast perspective', in J. Mitchell and O. Gower (eds) *Religion and the news*, Farnham: Ashgate, pp 79-87.

Lindsay, R. (2002) *Recognizing spirituality: The interface between faith and social work*, Crawley, WA: University of Western Australia Press.

McPhillips, K. (2017) '"Unbearable knowledge": Managing cultural trauma at the Royal Commission', *Psychoanalytic Dialogues*, vol 27, no 2, pp 130-46.

Prochaska, F. (2006) *Christianity and social service in modern Britain: The disinherited spirit*, Oxford: Oxford University Press.

Ranson, D. (2008) 'A service shaped by Catholic identity', in N. Ormerod (ed) *Identity and mission in Catholic agencies*, Strathfield, NSW: St Pauls Publications, pp 83-99.

Strickland, G.A., Welshimer, K.J. and Sarvela, P.D. (1998) 'Clergy perspectives and practices regarding intimate violence: A rural view', *Journal of Rural Health*, vol 14, no 4, pp 305-11.

Wendt, S. (2008) 'Christianity and domestic violence: Feminist poststructuralist perspectives', *Affilia*, vol 23, no 2, pp 144-55.

# NINE

# Religious literacy in welfare and civil society: A Nordic perspective

Annette Leis-Peters

## Introduction

While the concept of religious literacy has gained attention in the Anglo-Saxon world (Dinham and Francis, 2015), it is still new and hardly used in Nordic debates about religion. However, given the fact that the Nordic countries are often characterised as being at the forefront of secularisation (Welzel, 2013), one might anticipate that the Nordic countries should be at the forefront of debates about religious literacy.

In order to explore understandings of religious literacy in the Nordic countries, this chapter focuses particularly on the field of welfare and religion that has been recognised as an important arena to explore the changed role of religion between public and private spheres (Bäckström, 2014). The first part argues for the welfare perspective by presenting recent research in the sociology of religion that describes the interface between religion and the public sphere as Nordic complexity, and by referring to studies in Political Science highlighting the significance of religion for the formation and organisation of (European) welfare systems. This discourse about the role of religious organisations in welfare overlaps partly with the discourse about the role of civil society organisations in the Nordic welfare society. The second part explores Nordic studies about welfare and religion, pointing to a specific Nordic approach to the concept of religious literacy. The third part deepens this question with the help of two examples from Nordic case studies, a Swedish and a Norwegian one, that come from two recent Nordic research projects about the role of religious organisations in welfare and civil society. These examples illustrate that religious literacy should not only be thought of as the skill development of individuals and different groups of professionals, but also include an organisational perspective. Moreover, they also raise the question as to what kind of religious literacy is needed in Sweden and Norway.

## Nordic complexity

### *Changes in the religious landscape*

Nordic researchers in the field of religion tend to underline how complicated the religious situation in their countries is. The situation of religion in Sweden has been characterised as complex, based on more than 10 studies that were conducted with the aim of capturing the preconditions and possible effects of the transition of the Lutheran Church of Sweden from a state church to a free folk church in 2000 (Bäckström et al, 2004). On the one hand, Sweden can be used as an illustration of key arguments in the secularisation theory, such as the liberation of the state and the individual from the authority of the church, the privatisation of religion and the pluralisation of beliefs and worldviews. On the other hand, the Swedish research project shows that the formal separation of Swedish state and Swedish church has been put into practice relatively late and ineffectually compared to other Western countries, making the former state church a semi-official organisation. Surprisingly from an outside perspective, this new position gives the former state church more opportunities to engage in civil society and welfare than before, since it was legally impossible for the Church of Sweden to provide any welfare services competing with (other) public services until 2000 (Bäckström et al, 2004).

More than 10 years later, the Norwegian sociologist of religion Inger Furseth (2017) picks up the concept of complexity again when calling her book about recent changes in the religious landscape in the Nordic countries *Religious complexity in the public sphere*. This publication is the final analysis and summary of a Nordic research project, 'The Role of Religion in the Public Sphere' (NOREL), that was conducted in Denmark, Finland, Iceland, Norway and Sweden between 2009 and 2014. The project sought to trace changes in the interplay between religion and society in the period between the 1980s and 2013, which was a period of gradual membership decline for the Nordic majority churches. Membership of the Church of Sweden dropped from 90 to 66 per cent of the population between 1988 and 2013. Between 1980 and 2014, membership of the Church of Norway, which became more independent from the state in 2017, decreased from 88 to 75 per cent. The trends in the share of membership for Christian minority churches and registered faith communities outside Christianity give a more confusing picture. While Christian membership of minority churches decreased from 7.8 to 6 per cent in Sweden between 1988 and 2013, it grew in Norway from 3 to 6.6 per cent during the same period. Public statistics for the registered faith communities outside Christianity show also a clearer increase for Norway (from 0.1 to 3.2% between 1988 and 2014) than for Sweden (from 0.8 to 1.3%) between 1988 and 2013 (Furseth et al, 2017). Between 1990 and 2014, the percentage of inhabitants who were born outside Sweden increased from 9.2 to 15.9 per cent (Statistics Sweden, 2017), whereas in Norway, the percentage of residents born outside the country increased from 4.5 in to 13.8 per cent (Statistics Norway, 2014). That growing immigration numbers did not lead to a parallel membership growth in religious minority organisations may partly be explained by the different systems for registering and funding faith communities in these two countries.

Beginning with these demographic changes, the NOREL project looked specifically for shifts in the intersection of religion and state, religion and politics, religion and media and religion and civil society. In her conclusion, Furseth (2017) explains that even though the project took theories about secularisation and the return of religion as a point of departure, it turned to the concept of complexity in the final stage of the analysis because all the project's sub-areas needed the notion of complexity to describe the changes that they observed. While, for example, the general development of the role of religion in the Nordic countries during the last decades could be described as institutional differentiation (one of the main arguments in secularisation theory), the Nordic nation-states have at the same time still links to not only the majority churches, but also other faith communities in various and partly new ways. Religion has also become more visible in politics, the media and civil society. However, the growing visibility of religion must not be mistaken for gained importance and influence.

It is noticeable that whereas Nordic researchers nuance the picture and emphasise the complexity, European and global studies see the Nordic region as a clear example for countries in the forefront of individualisation, post-material values and secularisation, particularly for Sweden and Norway. Results from the European Value Study 2008-10 found that only 37 per cent of all Swedes and 54 per cent of all Norwegians believe in God, and that a clear majority from both countries (66% in Sweden and 54% in Norway) attend a religious service apart from baptisms, weddings and funerals less than once a year (Furseth et al, 2017). Does this mean that the majority of Nordic people just blank out religion from their daily life and their values?

In her recent study *Living simultaneity*, religious studies scholar Ann af Burén sought to explore the beliefs and practices behind the statistical numbers of the group that represents the majority in surveys about religion in Sweden. She concluded that it would be a false conclusion to classify 70 per cent of the Swedish population as non-religious just because they cannot be described as religious either. Instead, it is more accurate to characterise this group as semi-secular. In in-depth interviews with 28 respondents she found that semi-secular Swedes neither look actively for religious environments nor combine different religious elements into a personal religion. Furthermore, the ways that they relate to religion is so multifaceted that traditional ways of defining secularity or religiousness are insufficient. Af Burén introduces the concept of simultaneity to summarise her findings. Simultaneity includes individuality, autonomy and the ability to integrate different beliefs, values and practices. The respondents report that they have a 'normal' approach to religion, but actually the concept of simultaneity challenges dominant perceptions in the public, and partly also that research discourse that presupposes that beliefs and practices are either religious or secular. Af Burén's (2015) research can be read as a warning from simplifications and as a plea for paying attention to the complexity and the contradictions of religion and secularity in Sweden.

## *Seen and unseen in the Nordic welfare state*

Welfare is crucial for the Nordic states. That Nordic citizens trust in their strong states depends not least on the dominant role the state has in welfare. The complicated role of religion in the Nordic countries today is not a recent phenomenon, but can be ascribed to the historical circumstances of the development of the Nordic welfare state. Welfare researchers have repeatedly pointed to the connection between the universal social democratic welfare state with the aim of providing equal welfare services for all citizens, from cradle to grave, and Lutheran theology, the establishment of the Nordic state churches and secularisation. A universal welfare system presupposes a strong state that organises, funds, controls and provides welfare services. That state and Lutheran state church were closely intertwined since the Lutheran reformation in the 16th century has been assessed as an important precondition for this. Unlike in Catholic countries, no church–state conflict or cleavage hindered the establishment of the welfare state in the Nordic countries (Manow and van Kersbergen, 2009; Bäckström and Davie, 2010). Theologically, the doctrine of the two kingdoms allowed the Lutheran church to acknowledge the state as collaborator in the kingdom of God, even though it acted in the worldly realm (Ekstrand, 2011). Moreover, values such as autonomy of the individual, equality and social solidarity that are naturally connected to the social democratic welfare state today can easily be found in Lutheran theology (Wallman Lundåsen and Trägårdh, 2012).

However, emphasising the Lutheran tradition as the basis of the Nordic welfare state is misleading over the struggles between Nordic state churches and the state of the field of welfare. Historical case studies illustrate that when state and church started to dissolve gradually, and the state took over more and more welfare tasks (including school, healthcare, poor relief and social care) from the 1860s and until the mid-20th century, the state church leaders were either passive in the political debate (Anderson, 2009) or opposed the left-wing working-class ideology (Tønnessen, 2014) that the founders of the welfare state tried to realise. In return, the churches and faith-based organisations were not taken into consideration as providers of professional welfare services by the architects of the Nordic welfare state. There was only one area in which they were considered to be able to contribute: supporting their members in personal challenges and situations of existential crisis (Leis-Peters, 2014). This is an area that is clearly related to the private sphere.

Irrespective of whether the national churches are perceived as roots or as opponents of the social democratic welfare state, their contribution to professional welfare services is still rather limited. Like all faith communities they did not enter the scene of welfare provision to a considerable extent during the last two decades. This is surprising, since austerity in the welfare sector and the growing diversity that goes along with a greater variety of welfare needs made Nordic welfare policies reconsider the role of the voluntary sector, including faith communities. Together with other civil society organisations they have increasingly been welcomed as providers into an emerging welfare mix (Busch Zetterberg, 1996). However, there is no evidence that the share of civil society organisations in welfare provision has increased significantly in Sweden or Norway (Johansen, 2010; Sivesind, 2016) despite a number of political strategies or declarations that asked urgently for their participation in welfare. On the contrary, a long-term comparison of the share of diaconal institutions in different sectors of welfare and healthcare in Norway shows that there has been, for example, a constant decrease in involvement of diaconal institutions in almost all areas of welfare and healthcare since the 1980s (Angell, 2009). Exact numbers for all faith communities are hard to get because most studies look for the participation of civil society organisations in general without differentiating between the values and ideologies that they are based on. However, nothing indicates that faith communities in general and the Nordic majority churches in particular are exceptions in any way. Like the other civil society organisations, they are almost not involved in the provision of professional welfare services. This is true both for faith communities in a narrower sense and for religious organisations with a focus on professional welfare provision, such as diaconal institutions.

## Connecting religious literacy and Nordic research about welfare and religion

Despite religious literacy not being a widely used concept in the Nordic discourse about the role of religion in the public sphere, religious education scholar Kerstin von Brömssen (2013) concluded that religious literacy is a relevant approach to the interdisciplinary discourse about necessary literacy competences in democratic societies. According to her, religious literacy is needed to achieve citizenship in the field of religion, which is an important aspect of democratic society. However, she is mainly interested in religious literacy as a democratic competence that can be taught in school, and does not specify what competences and contents religious literacy or religious citizenship should consist of in her opinion. Although social and organisational aspects could be part of the approach that she suggests, the lack of reflection about religious literacy on an organisational level in her contribution indicates that she thinks mainly of religious literacy or religious citizenship as an approach for preparing (young) individuals for encounters of and with religion.

The British sociologists of religion Adam Dinham and Matthew Francis (2015) have situated religious literacy in a much broader context than religious education, arguing that it is best to talk about religious literacies in the plural, and that the concept refers to both religious and secular beliefs and practices in various settings within and outside of religious education, religious studies and the media. Crucial for religious literacies is the aim of improving the 'conversation about the category of religion and belief' (Dinham and Francis, 2015, p 14), as it is not possible to leave out religion when talking about the public sphere. Religion and belief are necessarily part of identities, practices and the physical landscape for both individuals and organisations. The examples that they give in their edited volume concern encounters between individuals who represent organisational settings and single individuals such as between social workers and clients, university staff and students or employers and employees.

There are some recent Nordic studies about how religion and beliefs are handled in encounters between clients/patients and professional welfare and healthcare workers, but none of them uses the concept of religious literacy actively and explicitly. These include a Norwegian survey about the attitudes and practices of social workers when coming across religion and spirituality in their interaction with clients (Vetvik, 2016); a Swedish project about religion in institutional care settings (Nordin and Schölin, 2011); and a research project about how dementia care professionals deal with the spiritual needs and religiosity of their patients (Ødbehr et al, 2014, 2015). Even an analysis of the guidelines of the Swedish National Agency on Education about how to handle Muslim headscarfs in schools could be considered as a contribution to this field (Borevi et al, 2016). All these studies observe what happens when individuals with religious or secular beliefs enter the public sphere by using professional welfare and care services.

The field of Nordic research about religion and welfare is broader and much more comprehensive than the field of the above-mentioned studies, but much of the research focuses on another level of encounter, namely, the organisational or meso level, that is, the interaction between organisations, and not between professional representatives of organisations and individuals. These include studies about the welfare activities of both faith communities and professional religious welfare providers, such as diaconal institutions. Often, the projects are qualitative, based on local case studies, and concentrate on one of the two categories. An exception is the quantitative study about welfare and Islam in Sweden. Sociologist Klas Borell and social work researcher Arne Gerdner (2011) conducted a representative survey among all Muslim congregations in Sweden. The project was initiated because social work students at Mid University in Northern Sweden felt that they were not well enough prepared for working in multicultural and multireligious contexts without knowledge about religion in general and Islam in particular. The survey found that Muslim congregations not only promote religion, but are also places of social encounter and support. Many Muslim congregations have among their members, for example, groups that support recently arrived immigrants or visit old and sick people and prisoners. Muslim congregations that engage in the social field also often say that they have well-established networks with other actors in society. However, the welfare activities that the Muslim congregation report about could be described as answering existential and individual needs, and may thereby be perceived as belonging to the private, and not the public, sphere. In contrast to Angell's (2009) comparison of diaconal institutions in Norway that found that the participation of religious actors in welfare is decreasing, Borell and Gerdner's (2011) research suggests that new religious actors are becoming involved in welfare provision in the Nordic countries.

As mentioned above, many of the studies of religion and welfare in the Nordic countries are case studies focusing on a single locality. These include some large projects funded by the European Commission: 'Welfare and Religion in a European Perspective' (WREP) (Bäckström et al, 2010); 'Welfare and Values in Europe: Transitions related to Religion, Minorities or Gender' (WaVE) (Molokotos-Liederman et al, 2017); and 'Faith-based Organisations and Social Exclusion in European Cities' (FACIT) (Elander and Fridolfsson, 2011).

The WREP project included eight Western European countries. In each country one municipality was chosen where the researchers asked majority church representatives, representatives of the municipality and the local population about the role of the majority church in welfare. One of the cross-cutting results is that there seems to be a European consensus when it comes to the task-sharing in welfare between the public sector and church. It is expected that the state should have the main responsibility for welfare while the church is welcome to assist. However, how much welfare involvement is desired from the church differs between the different countries (and the different welfare models that they represent). In the three Nordic countries that participated in the study (Finland, Norway and Sweden) expectations towards church activities in welfare were much more limited than, for example, in countries with conservative-corporative welfare systems such as Germany or Italy. The Nordic respondents were particularly hesitant towards professional rights-based welfare services. This could be interpreted as a wish for religious welfare activities in the private, but not in the public, sphere, even though the expectations towards the Nordic majority churches have grown during the last decade (Bäckström et al, 2010).

The WaVE project continued the research of the WREP project, conducting a second round of case studies in the same municipalities, but focusing on religious minority organisations instead of majority churches. In addition to the eight Western European countries, four post-Iron Curtain countries (Poland, Croatia, Latvia and Romania) were included in the project. This time, the case studies did not follow a paralleled design. Instead, the national team selected different thematic foci for their case studies. School social work, homework programmes and family centres were some of the case study themes that were chosen in the Nordic countries. A common pattern across all countries, and especially in the Nordic countries, was that religious minority organisations did not provide professional welfare services but rather helped individuals to handle existential needs that often had to do with keeping up culture, religion and family cohesion. These existential needs were many times also closely linked to expectations and duties that concerned the field of welfare. Again, the welfare contribution of the religious organisations seemed to be more a matter of the private than the public sphere (Fokas, 2017).

Sweden was the only Nordic country represented in the FACIT project in which the Swedish researchers studied how religious organisations dealt with social tensions and social exclusion in the three biggest and most multicultural cities in Sweden: Stockholm, Gothenburg and Malmö. The results are based on qualitative, and partly ethnographic, case study work in selected Muslim and Christian congregations in these cities. Similar to the quantitative findings of Borell and Gerdner (2011), religious minority organisations (such as Muslim congregations) were found to work as social meeting places and promote networking with the majority society, but these potentials depended strongly on the communication skills of single individuals with key positions in the organisation (Elander and Fridolfsson, 2011). As such, the studies indicate that the welfare engagement of religious minority organisations is not about the professional welfare service that citizens have a right to claim, but about responding to individual existential or social needs.

## The need for religious literacy at the organisational level

Even though the three European projects did not exclude intentionally religious welfare organisations that provide professional welfare services, it is interesting that these types of organisations are absent in almost all the Nordic case studies. From what the case studies describe, the welfare work of religious organisations can easily be summarised as supporting individuals with existential challenges and as being a platform for networking. The European projects show also that public representatives and the population in the Nordic countries are positive about religious organisations that answer to individual existential or social needs. What does this say about the role of religious organisations in welfare and about religious literacy at the organisational level? Is religious literacy not needed as long as the religious organisations keep to the private sphere? As two examples from recent Nordic research projects demonstrate, there is the need for religious literacy at the organisational level.

### *Welfare contribution of religious organisations for young people at the margins*

'Youth at the Margins' (YOMA) was a comparative study of the contribution of faith-based organisations to social cohesion in South

Africa and Nordic Europe that sought to understand the role and importance of faith-based organisations for young people at the margins. Six local case studies – four in South Africa and two in the Nordic countries – involved mapping interviews with young people, representatives of religious organisations and other local representatives in big cities, medium-sized cities and in rural areas. What distinguished this project from other projects about the welfare contribution of religious organisations in local communities was that it did not take all the social activities of the religious organisations into consideration, but focused only on their work with and for marginalised young people.

The Norwegian case study took place in the multicultural city district of Søndre Nordstrand, a suburb of Oslo that has a population of approximately 37,000. In 2014, when the study was conducted, the Lutheran majority church, the Church of Norway, had 12,440 members in four parishes in Søndre Nordstrand. This is less than one-third of the local population, while membership rates outside Oslo are usually more than 70 per cent. In addition to the Church of Norway, 14 other religious organisations were registered in the district, nine of which received public subsidies. As the aim of the case study was to mirror the multicultural and multireligious character of the city district, all 18 religious organisations that were active in the area were contacted. Only when it was not possible to establish contacts or when the religious organisations insisted that they had no activities for young people were no interviews conducted. The empirical data consisted of 17 interviews with representatives of 12 religious organisations and six focus group interviews with youth groups.

Most of the religious organisations had activities for young people and were aware of the problem of marginalised young people in the city district. Many also expressed that young people with social problems were welcome, and reported individual cases of young people who had been included by the religious organisation. But none of the religious organisations provided professional welfare services for young people with social problems, and only one of them focused specifically on young people at the margins. Moreover, religious organisations often shared media perceptions of who the marginalised young people were: 'the young people hanging on the street'. Therefore, some of them considered their youth activities as a way of keeping young people away from the bad influence of young people hanging around on the streets. Others saw their contribution at offering alternatives or safe places where young people could escape the dangers of the rough youth culture. Altogether, the religious organisations were an important social resource for some of the young people, but only for a minority among them who were mostly not socially marginalised (Holte et al, 2018).

Utilising Niklas Luhmann's (1995) system theory, one of the case study researchers, Bjørn Hallstein Holte (2017), analysed the interaction of the religious organisations with other local organisations in the city district, including the interactions between religious organisations and local secular organisations and between the religious organisations and organisations outside the city district. The contact between religious organisations and local secular organisations in general and religious organisations and public authorities in particular turned out to be rather limited and one-sided. Holte identified three main areas of cooperation in the material: first, the religious organisations invited representatives of the local child protection services to seminars on their premises with the aim of helping their members understand why the child protection services acted as they did. There are serious communication problems between the public Norwegian child protection services and people with a migration background who are afraid that their children will be taken out of the families. In this tense constellation, the religious organisations acted as a kind of intermediary. Second, the police paid regular visits to the religious organisations to talk about the situation of young people. Third, most of the religious organisations were invited to a so-called Forum for Dialogue and Cooperation that had been initiated by the local police after some tragic cases of neglect of children in the city district. The representatives of all involved religious organisations reported proudly about being a partner in this initiative.

Holte's analysis showed that the contacts between religious organisations and public authorities are rather limited in the field of work with marginalised young people in this city district. The religious organisations do not provide any professional services and are not perceived as equal partners by the public authorities. Even though almost all their representatives express that they are interested in supporting young people at the margins, they do not become visible in this field and are not invited to concrete activities by the public authorities either. Following Dinham and Francis (2015), this situation could be described as a conversation that lacks quality or as a lack of religious literacy at the organisational level.

## *Renewed Swedish Agency for Support to Faith Communities*

The second example comes from the NOREL project. The project itself did not focus on welfare, but in the Swedish case study welfare emerged as a dimension of public governance of growing religious diversity. The case of the Swedish Agency for Support to Faith Communities (SST) illustrates how much public funding and public attention affect the perception and work of religious organisations and their possibilities of contributing to welfare and to acting in the public sphere.

The SST was established in 1971 as a consequence of the preposition for state finance for independent faith communities (that is, outside the Church of Sweden) as part of the process of de-establishing the Swedish state church. The preparation held that all faith communities – and not only the established state church – should be entitled to financial support by the state. It suggested a positive and active equal treatment of all religious and worldview communities, and used the following three political arguments in order to motivate financial support for faith communities:

- service argument, that is, the obligation of the state to meet the needs of the citizens, among others religious and cultural needs;
- democracy argument, that is, the need of a variety of religions, worldviews and ideologies to maintain a vital democracy;
- value argument, that is, the value base that different religions and worldviews account for democracy (Myndigheten för stöd till trosssamfund, 2017a).

Since its founding, the SST has been responsible for distributing and administrating public financial support for faith communities, and has conducted this task with little public attention. It has given organisational contributions and support for certain clearly defined religious activities. Only faith communities that have applied and fulfilled the requirements are entitled to funding. Since Swedish registration authorities do not collect any statistical information about religion, the SST has, from its beginnings, been a very important source for data about the status of religion in Sweden.

Recently the SST has started to re-negotiate its role and to change its profile by developing into a more visible actor and becoming a professional expert in religious issues in the public sphere. Part of the new strategy is that the SST uses the data that it collects as part of its funding task to contribute to more knowledge about religion in Swedish society. In 2012 it re-designed it website and started a publication series about religion in Sweden, and the Director of SST has started a blog on the website where he is arguing for giving religion a more highlighted position in society (Myndigheten för stöd till trosssamfund, 2017b).

In the same period, the SST has been delegated several strategic tasks from the government. Since the late 1990s, after a discotheque fire in Gothenburg, the SST has been responsible for coordinating the work of faith communities in crisis situations. However, it was not until 2011 that the SST employed its own crisis coordinator and published an information booklet about the role of faith communities when crises arise (Myndigheten för stöd till trossamfund 2017c). The Swedish Parliament had already decided in the 1980s that faith communities outside the Church of Sweden should receive financial support for their activities in healthcare chaplaincy, and that the funding be provided by the SST. Consequently, the SST contributed to the establishment of Orthodox, Muslim and Buddhist healthcare chaplaincies at the beginning of the 2000s, but had to wait until 2013 to be mentioned in the government's budget papers for the first time (Myndigheten för stöd till trossamfund, 2017d). In 2014, the SST was delegated three new tasks by the government. It received public funding to organise courses in democracy and Swedish society for leaders of faith communities (Myndigheten för stöd till trossamfund, 2013). The SST was also commissioned to prepare guidelines for interfaith and multicultural councils (Socialdepartementet, 2013). Moreover, the SST got public funding to give information about the election year 2014 by using its contacts with religious organisations. While the SST is the official contact, the religious minority organisations in particular are considered to be able to reach out to groups in society that otherwise would not be reached by any information about the election (Myndigheten för stöd till trossamfund, 2014a).

Each of these initiatives signifies a change of attitude of the government and the public towards religious organisations that are increasingly perceived as 'a good force in society'. This is at least the title of an information booklet about religious organisations that was published in 2014 by the Ministry of Health and Social Affairs (Myndigheten för stöd till trossamfund, 2014b). The assumption that religious organisations are 'a good force in society' also resulted in a state-of-the-art report about the social activities of religious organisations that the Ministry of Health and Social Affairs commissioned (Socialdepartementet, 2015), which defined religious organisations as important welfare actors. It distinguished four different dimensions in the social activities of religious organisations: religious organisations as meaning-creating communities (covering the core activities of the religious organisations); religious organisations' unique contribution to public activities (focusing on chaplaincies in healthcare, prisons, the army and police); confessional alternatives to public services (focusing mainly on different pre-schools, schools and other educational institutions run by religious organisations); and religious organisations as actors in current social debates (focusing on the advocacy role of religious organisations). At first sight this seems like a comprehensive recognition of religious organisations in the field of welfare. However, most of the activities that are highlighted in this report relate to the existential needs of individuals, indicating that religious organisations are perceived as welfare actors in the private sphere, but not as professional welfare providers in the public sphere.

Over the last five years the SST has contributed to a public acknowledgement of faith communities as important resources in society in general and in welfare in particular. There seems to be a particular connection between the SST redefining its own role and the changed perception of faith communities in the public sphere. Was the positive attention for faith communities only possible because the SST took a stand as an advocate for the valuable contribution of faith communities in the public sphere? Was it necessary to have a public authority as intermediary for faith communities in the public? Is the re-negotiation of the role of the SST an example for a quality conversation about religion or religious literacy at the organisational level?

## Conclusion

The chapter started with the question, what kind of religious literacy is needed in the welfare societies in Sweden and Norway? This question presupposes that the concept of religious literacy needs to be contextualised. The Nordic countries are characterised by a high degree of secularisation combined with an ambivalent presence of religion. This makes religious literacy a highly relevant concept for the context. The field of welfare and religion was particularly fruitful to study and understand this Nordic complexity. Religion is at the same time one of the main roots of the Nordic welfare state and ignored as a provider of professional welfare services. This does not mean that religious organisations do not contribute to the area of welfare. They obtain public appreciation for answering individual existential needs – expertise in individual existential needs is perceived as an important role of religion in welfare by both representatives of public authorities and local populations. However, this welfare role belongs rather to the private than to the public sphere.

The lack of quality in conversation about religion or of religious literacy is a problem not least at the organisational level, that is, in the interaction between organisations. In the case study of a super-diverse city district in Oslo, the Forum for Dialogue and Cooperation was the only example of a successful conversation that actually includes religious organisations. The positive references of all religious organisations in the city district to this forum indicate how important this high-quality conversation is for them. The opposite case is the SST in Sweden. This shows that it is possible for a public institution to provide space for religious organisations in the public sphere.

The Nordic perspective highlights the organisational perspective in the discussion about religious literacy. In secular countries with a strong tradition of expelling religious organisations from the public to the private sphere, individual religious literacy is not enough. Religious literacy as a tool for improving the conversation about religion and as a concept for analysis has to integrate the level of organisations in its theoretical framework. Looking into the Nordic context and the field of welfare and religion points to the significance of an organisational perspective for high-quality conversations about religion or religious literacy.

## References

af Burén, A. (2015), *Living simultaneity: On religion among semi-secular Swedes*, Södertörns University (www.diva-portal.org/smash/get/diva2:800530/FULLTEXT01.pdf).

Anderson, K.M. (2009) 'The church as nation? The role of religion in the development of the Swedish welfare state', in P. Manow and K. van Kersbergen (eds) *Religion, class coalitions and welfare states*, Cambridge: Cambridge University Press, pp 210-35.

Angell, O.H. (2009) 'Institusjonsdiakoni i den norske velferdsstaten ['Institutional diaconia in the Norwegian welfare state'], in E. Aadland (ed) *Kan institusjoner elske? Samtidsessayer om diakonale virksomheter* [*Can institutions love? Present-age essays about diaconal services*], Oslo: Akribe, pp 31-49.

Bäckström, A. (2014) *Välfärdsinsatser på religiös grund. Förväntningar och problem* [*Welfare efforts with a religious basis: Expectations and problems*], Skellefteå: Artos & Norma.

Bäckström, A. and Davie, G. (2010) 'A preliminary conclusion: Gathering the threads and moving on', in A. Bäckström, G. Davie, N. Edgardh and P. Pettersson (eds) *Welfare and religion in 21st century Europe. Volume I: Configuring the connections*, Farnham: Ashgate, pp 183-97.

Bäckström, A., Edgardh Beckman, N. and Pettersson, P. (2004) *Religious change in Northern Europe. The case of Sweden*, Stockholm: Verbum.

Borell, K. and Gerdner, A. (2011) 'Hidden voluntary social work: A nationally representative survey of Muslim congregations in Sweden', *British Journal of Social Work*, vol 41, no 5, pp 968-79.

Borevi, K., Leis-Peters, A. and Lind, A.-S. (2016) 'Layers of inconsistency. A multidisciplinary analysis of the Swedish National Agency on Education's Guidelines on Muslim headscarf', in A.-S. Lind, M. Lövheim and U. Zackariasson (eds) *Religion, law and democracy. New challenges for society and research*, Lund: Nordic Academic Press, pp 179-98.

Busch Zetterberg, K. (1996) *Det civila samhället i socialstaten: Inkomstkällor, private transfereringar, omsorgsvård* [*The civil society in the social state: Income sources, private transfers, care services*], Socialstatsprojektet, Stockholm: City University Press.

Dinham, A. and Francis, M. (2015) 'Religious literacy: Contesting an idea and practice', in A. Dinham and M. Francis (eds) *Religious literacy in policy and practice*, Bristol: Policy Press, pp 3-26.

Ekstrand, T. (2011) 'Thinking theologically about welfare and religion', in A. Bäckström, G. Davie, N. Edgardh and P. Pettersson (eds) *Welfare and religion in 21st century Europe II: Gendered, religious and social change*, Farnham: Ashgate, pp 107-50.

Elander, I. and Fridolfsson, C. (2011) *Faith-based organisations and social exclusion in Sweden*, Leuven/Den Haag: Acco.

Fokas, E. (2017) 'Welfare and values in Europe: Insights drawn from a comparative cross-country analysis', in L. Molokotos-Liederman, A. Bäckström and G. Davie (eds) *Religion and welfare in Europe: Gendered and minority perspectives*, Bristol: Policy Press, pp 261-90.

Furseth, I. (2017) 'Secularization, deprivatization or religious complexity', in I. Furseth (ed) *Religious complexity in the public sphere: Comparing Nordic countries*, London: Palgrave Macmillan, pp 291-312.

Furseth, I., Ahlin, L., Ketola, K. Leis-Peters, A. and Sigurvinsson, B.R. (2017) 'Changing religious landscape in the Nordic countries, in I. Furseth (ed) *Religious complexity in the public sphere: Comparing Nordic countries*, London: Palgrave Macmillan, pp 31-80.

Holte, B.H. (2017) 'Religion and integration: Religious organisations' communication in the diverse city district of Oslo', Unpublished manuscript.

Holte, B.H., Leis-Peters, A., Angell, O.H. and Korslien, K. (2018) 'Us and them: Faith based organisations and youth on the streets in Søndre Nordstrand, Oslo, Norway', Unpublished manuscript.

Johanssen, O. (2010) *Tjäna eller tjäna? Om vård eller vinst. Privatisering av vård, omsorg, skola – vilka tar över?* [*To serve or to earn. About care or profit. Privatisation of nursing, social care, school – Who takes over?*], Stockholm: Famna.

Leis-Peters, A. (2014) 'Hidden by civil society and religion? Diaconal institutions as welfare providers in the growing Swedish welfare state', *Journal of Church and State*, vol 56, no 1, pp 105-27.

Luhmann, N. (1995) *Social systems* (translated by K. Bednarz and D. Baeker), Stanford, CA: Stanford University Press.

Manow, P. and van Kersbergen, K. (2009) 'Religion and the western welfare state: The theoretical context', in P. Manow and K. van Kersbergen (eds) *Religion, class coalitions and welfare states*, Cambridge: Cambridge University Press, pp 1-38.

Molokotos-Liederman, L., Bäckström, A. and Davie, G. (eds) (2017) *Religion and welfare in Europe: Gendered and minority perspectives*, Bristol: Policy Press.

Myndigheten för stöd till trossamfund [Swedish Agency for Support to Faith Communities/SST] (2013) *Demokratin behöver oss. Ett material för arbete med demokrati og mänskliga rättigheter i trossamfunden* [*Democracy needs us. Material for work with democracy and human rights in faith communities*], Stockholm: SST.

Myndigheten för stöd till trossamfund [Swedish Agency for Support to Faith Communities/SST] (2014a) 'SST ska jobba med valåret 2014' ['SST will work with the election year 2014'] (www.sst.a.se/nyheter/nyhetsarkivaktuellt/sstskalljobbamedvalaret2014.5.eb24cf614241a7f0892d0e.html).

Myndigheten för stöd till trossamfund [Swedish Agency for Support to Faith Communities/SST] (2014b) 'Trossamfunden – en god kraft i samhälle' ['Faith communities – A good source in society'] (www.sst.a.se/nyheter/nyhetsarkivaktuellt/trossamfundenengodkr aftisamhallet.5.38228ad4143b35110977082.html).

Myndigheten för stöd till trossamfund [Swedish Agency for Support to Faith Communities/SST] (2017a) 'Nämnden för statligt stöd till trossamfund' ['The board of state support for faith communities'] (www.sst.a.se/download/18.3e8d58c211f8378233080009349/ Uppfoljningrapport2.pdf).

Myndigheten för stöd till trossamfund [Swedish Agency for Support to Faith Communities/SST] (2017b) Direktören Åke Göranssons blogg [Director Åke Göransson's blog] (www.sst.a.se/kontakt/ake sblogg.4.11165b2c13cf48416deda9.html).

Myndigheten för stöd till trossamfund [Swedish Agency for Support to Faith Communities/SST] (2017c) 'SST og trossamfundens krisberedskap' ['SST and the emergency preparedness of faith communities'] (www.sst.a.se/krisberedskap.4.7f968fc211eeec933 de800012033.html).

Myndigheten för stöd till trossamfund [Swedish Agency for Support to Faith Communities/SST] (2017d) 'SST og den andliga vården innom hälso- och sjukvården' ['SST and spiritual care in the healthcare sector'] (www.sst.a.se/andligvard.4.55431e1f13f86263 d6a929.html).

Nordin, M. and Schölin, T. (2011) *Religion, vård och omsorg: mångkulturell vård i praktiken* [*Religion, care and nursing: Multicultural care in practice*], Malmö: Gleerups.

Ødbehr, L., Kvigne, K. Hauge, S. and Danbolt, L.J. (2014) 'Nurses' and care workers' experiences of spiritual needs in residents with dementia in nursing homes: A qualitative study', *BMC Nursing*, vol 12, no 13, pp 1-9.

Ødbehr, L., Kvigne, K. Hauge, S. and Danbolt, L.J. (2015) 'A qualitative study of nurses' attitudes towards and accommodations of patients' expressions of religiosity and faith in dementia care', *Journal of Advanced Nursing*, vol 71, no 2, pp 359-69.

Sivesind, K.H. (2016) 'Endring av fordelingen mellom ideelle, kommersielle og offentlige velferdstjenester i Skandinavia ['Changes in the distribution between value-based, commercial and public welfare services in Scandinavia'], in K.H. Sivesind (ed) *Mot en ny skandinavisk velferdsmodell? Konsekvenser av ideell, kommersiell og offentlig tjenesteyting for aktivt medborgerskap* [*Towards a new Scandinavian welfare model? Consequences of value-based, commercial and public service provision for active citizenship*], Oslo: Institutt for samfunnsforskning, pp 17-39.

Socialdepartementet [Ministry of Health and Social Affairs] (2013) 'Uppdrag angående handledning om interreligiösa och mångkulturella råd' ['Mandate for guidelines for interreligious and multicultural councils'] (www.regeringen.se/contentassets/e7113cf63ddf40e599e58b77a91f3622/uppdrag-angaende-handledning-om-arbete-med-interreligiosa-och-mangkulturella-rad-s20138355pbb).

Socialdepartementet [Ministry of Health and Social Affairs] (2015) *Trossamfundens sociale insatser: En preliminär undersökning* [*The social engagement of faith communities: A preliminary study*], Ds 2015:3, Stockholm: Fritzes.

Statistics Norway (2014) 'Immigrants and Norwegian-born to immigrant parents, 1 January 2014' (www.ssb.no/en/befolkning/statistikker/innvbef/aar/2014-04-24).

Statistics Sweden (2017) 'Summary of population statistics 1960-2016' (www.scb.se/en/finding-statistics/statistics-by-subject-area/population/population-composition/population-statistics/pong/tables-and-graphs/yearly-statistics--the-whole-country/summary-of-population-statistics/).

Tønnessen, A.V. (2014) 'The church and the welfare state in post-war Norway: Political conflicts and conceptual ambiguities' *Journal of Church and State*, vol 56, no 1, pp 13-35.

Vetvik, E. (2016) *Religion og livssyn i profesjonelt sosialt arbeid. Varierende praksis i klientarbeidet: inkludering, marginalisering og ekskludering. En survey om holdninger og handlinger i et Utvalg av Norske Sosialarbeidere* [*Religion and life stance in professional social work. Varying praxis in work with clients: Inclusion, marginalisation and exclusion. A survey on attitudes and activities among a sample of Norwegian social workers*], Oslo: VID Specialized University.

von Brömssen, K. (2013) 'Religious literacy: Är det et användvart begrepp i religionsdidaktisk/ -religionspedagogisk forskning? ['Religious literacy: Is this a useable term in research on the didactics of religion/pedagogics of religion?'], in B. Afset, K. Hatlebrekke and H.V. Kleive (eds) *Kunnskap til hva? Om religion i skolen* [*Knowledge of what? On religion in school*], Trondheim: Akademika, pp 117-43.

Welzel, C. (2013) *Freedom rising: Human empowerment and the quest for emancipation*, New York: Cambridge University Press.

Wallman Lundåsen, S. and Trägårdh, T. (2013) 'Social trust and religion in Sweden: Theological belief versus social organization', in J. de Hart, P. Dekker and L. Halman (eds) *Religion and civil society in Europe*, Dordrecht, Heidelberg: Springer, pp 109-24.

# PART 3:
# RE-IMAGINING THE FUTURE

# TEN

# Policy futures for religion and belief

Christopher Baker, Beth R. Crisp and Adam Dinham

## Introduction

Having outlined some of the main themes and trajectories that have emerged from this interdisciplinary enquiry into how religions and beliefs are being theorised and researched across the Arts and Humanities, it is now time to reprise the main implications for the benefit of policy audiences and practice. These include the contested role of religion within modern liberal states; the problem of violence that emerges from both religious and secular forms of exceptionalism; increasing de-sacralisation of the public sphere in politics, culture and education; the struggle of legal and policy frameworks to address new diversities and subjectivities; growing interest in spaces, landscapes and geographies of religious and spiritual practice; engagement with the ways in which these intersect with new political and civic forms of engagement; the blurring but also hardening of both religious and secular boundaries and identities; the search for new forms of ethical engagement and participation; the need for new understandings of how modernity and religion coexist and how this shapes public policy; the importance of understanding the nuance and complexity of the secular identity as well as the religious; the need for a new imagination of the public sphere; and the challenge of reimagining religion and belief, not only after the secular but after the postsecular too.

It is not yet clear how we sustain a renewed policy discourse that might address these issues. Our evidence suggests that every move into a more open and holistic framing of what the experience of being complexly religious, spiritual and secular might entail can be hijacked by well-worn tropes, binaries and stereotypes. On religion, these usually revolve around polarities of the secular vs sacred, private vs public and 'good' vs 'bad'. The challenge we have sought to address in this volume is to understand and respond to religion and belief in ways that engage with the ordinary cosmopolitan diversity they represent. The contributions in this volume suggest that a number of journeys are needed or are currently underway.

## Going beyond the secular and postsecular?

Perhaps the biggest and most difficult is the journey from ideas of the secular and postsecular to a conception of public spheres – and people – as continuingly sacred and secular. Perhaps the best way forward, supported by the approach of this volume, is to say that these still important categories remain, but they are gradually being subsumed within other conceptual frameworks that begin to flesh out the simultaneous tactics by which many people hold both secular and religious identities in increasingly blurred and complex ways. The growth of populism and nationalism, the desire for authenticity and re-enchantment, all generated as a response to new global uncertainties and deep change, have at their heart new configurations of the religious, the secular and the spiritual. The postsecular is a concept that has succeeded in opening up new spaces of critical discussion around the fluid, blurred and contested nature of the public sphere. However, it has also sharpened and polarised the debate because of its associations with a sort of denunciation of Western notions of secularism with its linear framing of growth and decline. This volume points instead to an understanding of religion and belief in terms of mutation and change.

What is clear across most of the contributions is that religion, belief and the secular continue to adapt to each other and to frame each other – whether it be the deformalisation of religion from institutional to profane spaces to the embracing of humanist and 'non-religion' searches for deeper meaning and authenticity. There is no trajectory to a vanishing point, and simplistic assertions of secularity risk violent kickbacks from religious-based terrorism such as the incident at the offices of Charlie Hebdo. At the same time, accepting that religion and belief persist does only half the job; realising that religion and the secular are not two sides of a battle is the rest.

## From law to talk

As Lucy Vickers, Lori Beaman and Mark Brett show, law is one of the public spheres in which religion and belief most prominently meet these binary secular assumptions. From a UK context, Vickers explores the possibilities of the principle of proportionality, namely, that 'the question of whether a restriction on religion or belief is acceptable is assessed by whether it is a proportionate means of achieving a legitimate aim.' She sees this as a far more inclusive and non-binary approach to the public expression of religion and belief than the more prominent framework of 'reasonable accommodation', which, in some senses, reproduces the binary – a them and an us, religious or secular.

Brett, to some extent, takes a countercultural stance to this. He argues, from an Australian context, that one of the progressive dividends from the postsecular debate is the re-admittance of foundational theological and philosophical values and principles to social policy (as argued for by Habermas among others). He thinks this policy turn back to Theology could enable a return to valuable Christian defences of the natural rights of Indigenous peoples and therefore to the restoration of land rights, for example. He also envisages a critical and holistic appreciation of the doctrines of creation found across religious traditions, which could potentially legally underpin the rights of non-human animals in ways that build links with Indigenous spiritualities. In doing so, he suggests that Australian policy could begin to address the needs and rights of Indigenous people by acknowledging, in legal principles, the need for engagement with the 'complex webs of spirituality' that lie at the heart of a 'postsecular' Australian identity.

Beaman, on the other hand, stresses both the challenges and opportunities created by increasing fluidity and diversity. On the upside, she perceives in this a pressure for majoritarian religion in Canada (that is, Christian) to be seen more as part of wider culture. More challengingly, she also sees the risk of reproducing the notion of religion and belief as somehow separate to the rest of what goes on in the public sphere. Either way, she concludes that previously defined boundaries between the religious and the secular are becoming more diffuse, and the law is possibly becoming more adept at recognising this.

As it stands, however, the law is still a sphere with prominent responsibility for settling the challenges posed. It has been something of a lightning rod for the difficulties that inhere, hence the many cases it has sought to address on issues such as equal marriage, and visible manifestations of religion and belief in the workplace. A rights-based approach to religion and belief, focused on the principles of equality and freedom, is likely to result in a turn to those rights. It may repeatedly succeed in settling disputes on the basis of the facts that present, but the question remains whether it points the way to resolutions in similar or different disputes next time. In this sense law is revealed as inadequate to the task of negotiating, as opposed to settling, disputes in contexts of religion and belief diversity, although as guarantors of them it is at the same time essential. Spaces of dialogue and understanding are emerging as critical alternatives that might pre-empt the turn to law.

## From risk to opportunity, from good/bad to 'just is'

Connected to this legal-sphere journey is one in policy-making too, in which there are signs of a re-balancing in terms of opportunity as well as risk. Both are already implicit in policy that frequently looks both ways without always knowing it – constructing faith groups as heroes in relation to community and service provision, and as villains in relation to extremism. It is not only policy that is often perverse in this way; this applies to most policy arenas. But in relation to religion and belief it also reproduces the binary of 'good' and 'bad' religion, which in practice pains and confuses people of religion and belief who frequently experience both policy messages at once.

A key aspect of moving on will be an opening up of ideas of what counts as religion and belief, and a jettisoning of the expectation that it will be either good or bad. This will enjoin a concurrent shift from the binary of 'proper' and 'fake' religion and belief too. If society is neither simply sacred nor secular, so, too, are people neither simply religious or non-religious. They may be complexly both, or complexly neither, and new thinking tells us that religion and belief identities may be highly fluid anyway, changing within the same person from day to day, and even from moment to moment. Religion and belief without hierarchies, structures, leaders, doctrines and followers are difficult for policy, which frequently wants identifiable people, ideas and institutions with which to engage. Neither policy nor law will find it easy to engage with informal, fluid religion and belief without obvious normativities or values with which to engage. What must it provide to whom, and how and where? And how will disputes be articulated and resolved?

This creates a space for religious literacy as a vehicle for connecting traditional and apparently exotic forms of religion and belief to concrete practices. It also releases policy and practice from the fallacy of believing that it needs to learn the A-Z of a faith tradition in order to engage. This theme is expanded by Annette Leis-Peters and Beth Crisp. Leis-Peters, from a Nordic perspective, compares the growing research on the impact of religion on the welfare structures of both Norway and Sweden as a response to growing diversity and austerity. The roots of these welfare structures are historically religious, and religious groups still provide large amounts of social welfare, and yet, by and large, these religious roots are still seen as irrelevant. Leis-Peters suggests that when institutional bodies (as opposed to individual citizens) take the time and trouble to acknowledge and publicly explore the praxis of religious groups in society, this has a demonstrably beneficial impact on the planning, delivery and integration of welfare services across different sectors and partnerships. Crisp similarly suggests that, while still potentially problematic, the 're-discovery' of religion and belief within social worker training in Australia challenges out-dated and often overly-cautious professional assumptions regarding both the positionality and vocation of social workers themselves, and also their clients. While this approach will not be the panacea to solve deep-seated challenges to social care policies, she argues that not to re-imagine the role of religion and belief in the experiences of both social workers and their clients will be even more problematic.

## From irrelevant or dangerous to public sources of wisdom

Key to re-imagining is a new understanding that holding deep beliefs, values and worldviews is not the prerogative of religious people, but is intrinsic to human flourishing. Research on this explores a range of positions and worldviews under the label 'no religion', and this sets religion, belief and no religion on a spectrum of repositories of wisdom, insight and meaning-making with or without god(s), doctrines or theologies. This is a theme implicitly developed by all our contributors, but addressed particularly in the chapters by Lori Beaman, Beth Crisp, and Paul Cloke and Andrew Williams. It connects fundamentally with a renewed sense, emerging in reaction to several decades of neoliberal influence, that public life, civil society and governance are in need of being reconnected to deep narratives and imaginaries that sustain a practical and inclusive vision of the common good. Both religious and non-religious beliefs and traditions may have a shared role in this task – both in the imagining of a fairer and more just society, but also in new and creative forms of self-care, community, partnership and co-production to help bring this practically about (Featherstone et al, 2009; Calhoun, 2016).

To have beliefs, values and worldviews that shape and motivate action in the public sphere is not unusual and has sometimes been called 'spiritual capital' (see Baker and Miles-Watson, 2008). The challenge is for policy to move to a fuller recognition of values and beliefs – both religious and non-religious – in ways that do not get stuck in outdated binaries of secular or religious. This might counteract the risk of pathologising religion in social policy and practice and recognise the presence or absence of religious and non-religious beliefs as being as ordinary as other common forms of diversity within communities.

## From text on a page to performed space

This volume also indicates a 'spatial turn' across all the disciplines considered towards an embodied, embedded and performative understanding. In this, religion and belief are seen as diffuse across the public sphere by 'de-formalising' from traditional (and in some ways declining) institutional and designated spaces and spilling out into other public/'secular' spaces of media, culture and politics. This shift is likened in Chapter 2 to a 'Jacuzzi' where religion and belief are bubbling up everywhere rather than being contained within the directed flow of a 'shower'. Two chapters in this volume address this spatial turn specifically. From a Religious Studies perspective, Oliver Scharbrodt explores the multitemporal and spatial ways in which modern religion and belief identities are created and sustained, and how adept they are at thriving and flourishing in contemporary modernity. He observes how Twelver Shii communities in the UK negotiate local public space to their own advantage with reference to national politics, transnational connectivities (back in Iran) and 'supra-locative religious imaginaries that transcend the local, the national and the transnational.' His research shows the intentionally sophisticated way in which religious identity engages with so-called secular public space.

On a more existential and material level, Paul Cloke and Andrew Williams highlight an increased interest in geographies of the sacred, spiritual landscapes, and psycho-spiritual geographies. These range from a renewed public interest in visiting sacred and religious sites and undertaking pilgrimages to how ideas of the transcendent and spiritual map on to the experiences of young people experiencing precarity in Glasgow. While the implications for policy of this 'spatial turn' remain perhaps more implicit than explicit, nevertheless it highlights the importance of moving beyond 'lived', 'text-based' and/ or legalistically framed understandings of religions and beliefs to those that are spatially informed and performed as well. Policy needs to be guided to a better understanding of how religions and beliefs are active in helping 'produce' the public sphere in which they take part, and how their progressive practices of hospitality and tolerance on the ground are often missed because they do not 'fit' into dominant policy stories that foreground radicalisation or inclusion, and therefore do not register as significant.

## From homogeneous tradition to fluid identity

Despite often being often treated as homogeneous, notions of religion and belief (or non-religion and non-belief) are short-hand for a complex array of potentially disparate, even at times seemingly contradictory, phenomena. Rituals, beliefs and practices associated with religious practice may reflect personal piety or may be enacted for social or cultural reasons associated with one's individual or communal identity. Similarly enactments of a seemingly non-religious nature performed beyond the realm of religious institutions or communities must be recognised as enabling the development and maintenance of identity, which may or may not include religion. Yet in public policy and practice, there is commonly limited capacity to engage and work effectively with the diversity and fluidity of individuals, groups or organisations for whom lived religion, belief and non-belief are integral to their sense of identity. While individuals and communities rightfully expect policy-makers and professional practitioners to have a degree of expertise, such expectations are often not realised when it comes to matters of religion and belief (Crisp, 2015). The challenges for professional training and regulation are many.

## From proxy to named

There is a long history within public policy and professional practice of not naming religion, but hiding it within seemingly more acceptable euphemisms and apologetic proxies. Hence 'spirituality' is often preferred to 'religion', even when the latter is technically more correct (Hay and Nye, 2006). Consequently, the importance of the explicitly religious dimension of the lives of individuals and communities can too easily be disregarded. Similarly, subsuming religion under the banner of 'multiculturalism' not only raises the potential for religion to be rendered exotic and considered only of relevance to minority ethnic groups rather than to all members of a society. Likewise, while 'multifaith' initiatives can break down much of the suspicion about other religions and enable synergies to be explored, such efforts are only authentic when the contribution of each religion also receives recognition for its unique contributions to society.

There are also fundamental issues of transparency and accountability as religion, belief and non-belief actors participate increasingly across the public sphere. Resort to Habermas' 'public reasons' prevents us from naming the religion, belief and non-belief that is there, and therefore inhibits the ability to understand what it does, and to hold it to account. Comfortable proxies risk obscuring the realities and undermine the ability to understand what is on offer, engage with it and challenge.

In the end, failure to engage in the language of religion, belief and non-religion can render it difficult to effectively engage with pivotal individuals and organisations around public policy initiatives. For example, efforts to address gender-based violence within religious communities have been most promising when they have engaged with the religious beliefs and language of the target group (Holmes, 2012). This demands a deep re-imagining of religion and belief and the secular, and the relationship between them. More than this, it requires the forensic outworking in policy and practice of these new ways of thinking.

## The beginning, not the end

The study of religion, belief and non-belief is arguably more relevant than ever in the 21st century, but if its contribution is to be realised, the questions and approaches we have introduced in this volume must be addressed. Although marking the end of the Re-imagining Religion and Belief for Policy and Practice project, this volume is much more akin to a beginning than an end in respect of how religion and belief are manifesting in public policy and practice. The processes, methods and dialogues that we have described, and the themes we have drawn out in this concluding chapter, not only demonstrate that new understandings of religion, belief and non-belief in the public sphere are possible, but will also hopefully stimulate further explorations in other disciplines, sectors and settings and in respect of other social issues and constellations. This includes the constellations within the academy that continue to favour siloed discipline-specific approaches to knowledge, such that there are those that 'do religion' (namely, Theology, Religious Studies, History and, at a push, Literature) and those that do not. Yet there are many signs of a greater preoccupation with religion and belief outside those disciplines as they notice them through their own lenses in relation to migration, diversity, extremism, welfare and others. The epistemologies that subtly underpin their different perspectives on religion and belief are central to the task of re-imagining. How can the Arts, Humanities and Social Sciences move from secular, functionalist, rationalist, empiricist siloes, and their attendant methodologies, to whatever is emerging after the postsecular, let alone the secular? Then, how can they share what they discover with policy-makers, the professions, workplaces and the public sphere? This is the challenge ahead.

## References

Baker, C. and Miles-Watson, J. (2008) 'Exploring secular spiritual capital: An engagement in religious and secular dialogue for a common future', *International Journal of Public Theology*, vol 2 no 4, pp 442-64.

Calhoun, C. (2016) *Religion, government and the public good*, Manchester: William Temple Foundation.

Crisp, B.R. (2015) 'Religious literacy and social work: The view from Australia', in A. Dinham and M. Francis (eds) *Religious literacy: Enhancing understanding and cooperation*, Bristol: Policy Press, pp 207-26.

Featherstone, D., Ince, A., Mackinnon, D., Strauss, K. and Cumbers, A. (2012) 'Progressive localism and the construction of political alternatives', *Transactions of the Institute of British Geographers,* vol 37, no 2, pp 177-82.

Hay, D. and Nye, R. (2006) *The spirit of the child* (revised edn), London: Jessica Kingsley Publishers.

Holmes, S. (2012) *Northern Interfaith Respectful Relationships: Project report* (www.vichealth.vic.gov.au/~/media/ResourceCentre/PublicationsandResources/PVAW/Sharing%20the%20evidence_NIRR%202012.pdf?la=en).

# Afterword: A global challenge

## Grace Davie

I was delighted to be part of the residential colloquium that constituted the second element of the project that lies behind this book (see p 16). On the final day, I (together with Professor James Beckford) was invited to make some concluding reflections. I can see from the preceding chapters that a number of the themes that I introduced at this juncture have been taken up by those who were present. Selectively these include the need to be aware that shifts in perception, just as much as reality, are crucial to our understandings of the post-secular; that religious literacy is best considered as a plural construct; and that context matters hugely in our understanding of these issues.

In this short Afterword I want to place the colloquium, and the project of which it is part, in a broader perspective. The colloquium took place in May 2015. Shortly before this I had accepted an invitation to become a coordinating lead author (CLA) for the chapter on religion in a project entitled the 'International Panel on Social Progress' (IPSP).[1] Thus the two activities ran side by side. The scale was different but the parallels between them became ever more striking as the months passed.

## International Panel on Social Progress

The IPSP brought together more than 200 scholars from a wide range of disciplines and from many different parts of the world to assess and synthesise the state-of-the-art knowledge that bears on social progress across a wide range of economic, political and cultural questions.[2] The goal was to provide the target audience (individuals, movements, organisations, politicians, decision-makers and practitioners) with the best expertise that social science can offer.

The process – to a significant extent modelled on the Intercontinental Panel on Climate Change (IPCC) – was a long one. A team of five to ten authors took responsibility for each of the 22 chapters, working under the direction of the two CLAs. Following IPCC practice, an initial draft of the chapters was posted online for several months in the latter part of 2016 in order to collect comments from the widest possible audience and to allow the authors to read and respond to each other's work. A second draft was prepared with the comments in mind. The report as a whole was published in 2018 (*Rethinking society for the 21st century*, IPSP, 2018), alongside a summary version for a more general audience (Fleurbaey et al, 2018).

There are two introductory and two concluding chapters in the full report. The remaining 18 are divided into three sections: economic, political and cultural. Unsurprisingly the chapter on religion – entitled 'Religions and social progress: Critical assessments and creative partnerships' – falls into the last of these categories, along with the material on cultural change, the pluralisation of families, global health and the parameters of human living, education, and belonging and solidarity. Social progress, the key to the whole enterprise, is defined in Chapter 2, in which the notion of a compass is deployed as a metaphor. A compass sets the line of travel, but the map in question is complex and the destination elusive: what is considered progress in one situation may be differently assessed in another.

## The chapter on religion

The first step was to build the team, bearing in mind that we needed expertise from different disciplines, different world faiths and different global regions. Above all, we needed hands-on experience in empirical work in order that our text might be fully grounded in the realities of religion as they exist in different parts of the world. At the same time we had to find a discourse – a literacy – that related these realities to the concept of social progress as this was understood by the project as a whole. And just like the team engaged in *Re-imagining religion and belief*, we had to find ways of making this speak to a diverse readership, both inside and outside the academy.

### Defining the task and defining religion

The first meeting of the IPSP authors (including ourselves) took place in Istanbul in August 2015. It was a learning experience in every sense of the term. Not only was this the first time that the chapter team had come together (some of them travelling many thousands of miles), it was also the moment when we appreciated that significant sections of the social-scientific mainstream were hesitant about the relationship between religion and social progress as we were learning to understand this. This hesitancy took two forms: either religion was irrelevant (that is, no longer of significance), or it was negatively perceived – in other words, inimical to social progress. The fact that religion was (or more accurately was deemed to be) 'back' was therefore a problem.

In the 48 hours that we spent together, we worked hard on finding ways to counter these at best partial, and at worst inaccurate, views, starting with a clear definition of religion itself. Escaping the limitations of a purely Western perspective was the first step. We argued that religion is more – much more – than the broad range of institutions and beliefs traditionally recognised by social science; it is, rather, a very much larger cultural domain that encompasses the beliefs and practice of the vast majority (well over 80%) of the world's population (Johnson et al, 2016). Religion is a lived, situated and constantly changing reality, and has as much to do with navigating everyday life as it does with the supernatural. It follows that secularity should be considered an equally fluid entity, whose distinction from religion will vary from place to place – a division decided more by the context in question that by pre-determined categories.

From this starting point we developed our approach to the relationship between religion and social progress. Our task was to scour the available literature in order to document our case, but we began from the belief that neither good nor ill could be assumed from the outset. We had rather to look case-by-case in different social and cultural domains, and in different parts of the world, to see what was happening on the ground. We were well aware that particular kinds of religion were perceived negatively, sometimes rightly so. Without doubt religion can take forms that are destructive of people and places. Elsewhere, however, religious individuals and religious communities are manifestly associated with the health and wellbeing of their respective societies – an entirely positive feature.

## *Expanding the field*

In order to get a grip on the agenda we worked 'upwards' from the micro to the macro. Specifically, we began with the most intimate of human relationships (that is, those that relate to gender, sexuality and the family), appreciating that these have been moulded from time immemorial by religious rules, rituals and prohibitions. But here, as elsewhere, it is important to set aside an over-simple binary between secular progress and religious reaction – the reality is infinitely more complex. The focus on everyday lived religion was a valuable corrective in this respect. It pointed us to a multidisciplinary literature that documents the ways in which men, women and young people negotiate their very personal lives. It is clear that they accept some of the limitations that derive from religion but question others, and extract from these complex negotiations the means to confront the vicissitudes of life.

## AFTERWORD: A GLOBAL CHALLENGE

For example, certain forms of conservative religion undoubtedly resist progress, notably when 'fundamentalist' types of religion challenge (at times violently) what they deem to be the sexual 'decadence' associated with the West. Less well known are the subtle ways in which (mostly) women deploy or even subvert their religiously ascribed roles to construct fulfilling lives both for themselves and their families. Yet other women advance their cause in religiously based reform movements or alternative spiritualities, rather than – or as well as – secular substitutes. It is important, finally, to recall that the divisions between conservative and more liberal approaches run through the world's religions rather than between them – a theme that pervades our chapter.

The subsequent sections deal with political issues. The first addresses the question of diversity – looking (a) at its shape and forms in the late modern world and (b) at its governance. A constructive starting point lies in the recognition that *religious* diversity is part and parcel of a broader agenda, but that it has particular characteristics. Religious differences, for example, are likely to raise more intractable questions than variations in taste or style. Equally central is an awareness that diversities exist, largely (if not exclusively) because of the movement of people, both forced and unforced. An overall increase in religious diversity should not, however, be assumed. In some global regions (the modern Middle East, for instance) it declines as religious minorities are forced to leave; in others it grows as significant numbers of migrants arrive (West Europe); and in yet other parts of the world it has been there for centuries (Southeast Asia). Whatever the case, it is important to note the two-way flows between religion and migration. On the one hand, religions inspire, manage and benefit from the migration process but on the other, they are shaped and moulded by the dislocations of populations that inevitably ensue. You cannot have one without the other.

The consequences require careful management: migration is a hot political issue. For which reason, we reflected carefully on the various forms of governance discovered in this field and the debates that surround them. These include the pros and cons of multiculturalism, of diverse forms of secularism, and of democracy itself. We recognised, however, that there are deeper questions to address: those that probe the ways in which religiously diverse people do not simply co-exist but flourish in each other's company. We discovered, for example, that 'street-level ecumenism' (working side by side) is often more effective than a dialogue between elites. Lori Beaman – a contributor to the present volume – has developed this point in more detail, asking what might be discovered if we turned our attention to the success stories of diverse living rather than to points of conflict (Beaman, 2017). Such an approach drives us back once again to the realities of lived religion in addition to its official formulations.

The second of our political sections confronts directly the much talked-of connections between religion and conflict. The core argument is easily stated. To ask whether religion – or certain forms of religion – cause conflict or violence is not the most helpful approach. Much more constructive are enquiries that look systematically at the circumstances in which a violent outcome is likely. Contestation over physical spaces is one such, as is an excess of regulation that leads all too often to negative attitudes towards minorities. Even more important is the considerable evidence that weak or failed states (and the fragile economies associated with them) encourage – by default – violent and authoritarian attempts to restore order. Some of these are religiously inspired.

There is, however, another side to this coin. Clearly there are situations in which religion becomes entangled with violence, but it is equally a resource for peace-making. This can be seen in the attention to values (those associated with justice or righteousness) promulgated by all the world faiths; it can also be expressed organisationally. Both dimensions are illustrated in the local and concrete – in, for example, the sensitive management of particular sacred spaces – and in the deep expertise of global movements such as the Sant'Egidio Community, the World Council of Churches, and (to give but one American example) the Interfaith Dialogue and Peacebuilding Program at the US Institute of Peace. It is equally clear that religious actors are often critical players in post-conflict situations: good examples can be found in South Africa or Northern Ireland.

The relationship between religion and human rights offers a linking theme in this respect. The concept of human rights has become a defining discourse in the management of diversity, in the resolution of conflict and in the fair distribution of resources. Across all of these domains, however, the relationship between religion and human rights is differently regarded: from active advocacy at one end of the spectrum to open hostility at the other. There are those who draw from Article 18 of the United Nations (UN) Declaration on Human Rights to uphold the freedom of religion and belief as a fundamental and universally applicable human right; there are others who see the demands of religion and religious people as inimical to an alternative range of freedoms (those, for instance, of free speech, of women and of LGBTI communities). The existence of a UN Special Rapporteur on Freedom of Religion and Belief is indicative of a determination to find a way forward not only in places where diverse religious and secular norms are valued, but also in places where they are likely to come into conflict – gender-specific abuses being a case in point.

There are two further substantive sections in the IPSP chapter. The first picks up a theme that runs right through this volume in that it deals with the place of religion in the wellbeing of individuals and communities. Particular attention is paid to welfare, education and healthcare. A striking example will be taken to illustrate the approach. Faced with the seeming impasse between secular health professionals and faith-based initiatives in parts of the developing world, a series of contributions in *The Lancet* (2015) offers an evidenced-based way forward. The emphasis is on partnership, arguing that secular and faith-based organisations *can* work together even when there are areas of disagreement regarding policy and practice. The crucial point is to ascertain exactly what these are – and thus to establish not only what cannot be done in partnership, but the (normally much greater) areas of work that are able to be shared. The need is such that it is unwise to rule out significant resources on principle. Not all partnerships with religious organisations are advisable but many are – a theme pursued in some detail.

One further area requires attention – that is, the role of faith-based organisations in caring for the earth itself (the final step in our ascending scale). Unsurprisingly, given its genesis, a number of chapters in the IPSP report engage growing concerns about the environment and the role of social, as well as natural, science in understanding these better. Our task was more specific: namely, to draw attention to the place of religious groups in this enterprise. Again a single example captures the potential. *Laudato Si'* – the second encyclical of Pope Francis – was published in 2015; it has become a defining moment in the debate about climate change (Francis, 2015).

There are two reasons why the content and significance of *Laudato Si'* can hardly be overstated. First, the encyclical draws on established scientific research to deliver a powerful *ethical* message: that deprived communities will suffer disproportionately from the changes taking place. And second, the 'constituency' is vastly expanded. Put differently, the moral authority and popularity of the Pope will ensure a readership (and thus an impact) that scientific papers can only dream of – a fact recognised as much by scientists as by theologians and nicely exemplified by the leader entitled 'Hope from the Pope' published in *Nature* (2015).

## Policy-making

The concluding paragraphs of our IPSP chapter took the form of an action toolkit, which found its rationale in a set of cross-cutting themes that ran right through our material. These include the *persistence* of religion in the modern world (religion is neither vanishing nor resurgent); the importance of context in discerning outcomes (both positive and negative); the urgent need to enhance cultural competence (not least religious literacy) in different parts of the world; the significance of religion in initiating change; and the gains that accrue from effective partnerships. Not all of these can be pursued here, but the following stand out. First is the continuing need for assessment and – where necessary – constructive criticism, bearing in mind that social progress not only evolves but looks different in different places. Second are the demonstrable benefits of well-judged partnerships, noting that 'well-judged' is the crucial word in this assertion. In a sentence taken from the abstract of our chapter, Nancy Ammerman puts it thus:

> ... researchers and policy-makers pursuing social progress will benefit from careful attention to the power of religious ideas to motivate, of religious practices to shape ways of life, of religious communities to mobilize and extend the reach of social changes, and of religious leaders and symbols to legitimate call to action.

Not only is she is right, but her summary echoes many of the core themes of *Re-imagining religion and belief*. Both the team involved in the production of this book and the team engaged in the chapter on religion in the IPSP report had the same underlying aim: on the one hand, to grasp the essence of religion and how this operates in the everyday lives of countless individuals, groups and communities in different parts of the world, and on the other, to work out the consequences for both policy-makers and policy-making in late modern societies. Connecting the two requires not only careful documentation but also innovative thinking. Specialists in religion and belief are already engaged; their colleagues in the mainstreams of social science must resist the temptation to drag their feet.

## Notes

[1] I should add that the IPSP process required two CLAs (from different parts of the world) to work alongside each other in each chapter team. I was honoured when Nancy Ammerman, a distinguished sociologist of religion from Boston University, agreed to join me in this task.

[2] See www.ipsp.org and www.ipsp.org/downloads for more information regarding the background and working methods of the IPSP. Contributing authors are listed, chapter by chapter.

## References

Beaman, L.G. (2017) *Deep equality in an era of religious diversity*, Oxford: Oxford University Press.

Fleurbaey, M., with Bouin, O., Salles-Djelic, M.-L., Kanbur, R., Nowotny, H. and Reis, E. (2018) *A manifesto for social progress: Ideas for a better society*, Cambridge: Cambridge University Press.

Francis (2015) *Laudato Si': On care for our common home* (http://w2.vatican.va/content/francesco/en/encyclicals/documents/papa-francesco_20150524_enciclica-laudato-si.html).

IPSP (International Panel on Social Progress) (2018) *Rethinking society for the 21st century*, Cambridge: Cambridge University Press.

Johnson, T., Grim, B. and Zurlo, G. (eds) (2016) *World religion database*, Leiden: Brill.

*Lancet, The* (2015) 'Faith-based health care', vol 386, no 10005.

Nature (2015) 'Hope from the Pope', *Nature*, vol 522, no 7557, p 391.

# Index

## A

al-Abadi, Haider, 66
abortion, 111, 133
af Burén, A., *Living simultaneity*, 148-9
Al-Khoei Foundation, 64-5
*Alberta v Hutterian Brethren of Wilson Colony*, 100
*Amselem* case, 99-100
Anthropology, 18-20
Asher's bakery case, 83, 88
assisted death, 111
atheism, 103, 109
 *see also* non-religion
Australia
 child abuse and neglect, 124, 132-3
 health and welfare services, 132
 human rights discourse, 118, 126
 legal system fragmentation, 117
 *Mabo* case, 117-18
 religion and class, 131-2
 settler colonialism, 115-16, 119
*Azmi v Kirklees Metropolitan Borough Council*, 79

## B

Baptists, 121, 125
belief *see* religious belief
*Big M Drug Mart* case, 98-9
bin Talal, Hassan, 64
Bonello, Justice, 105-6
Brent, Twelver Shii Islam, 63-70
Brexit referendum, 6, 24, 65
British Asian diaspora, 62-3
*Bull & Anor v Hall & Anor*, 82, 88

## C

Canadian Charter of Rights and Freedoms, 98, 103, 108-9
*Carter v Canada*, 111
Catholics, Catholic-Cubans in Miami, 60, 61
*Chamberlain v Surrey School District*, 111-12
children
 child protection in Norway, 157
 church involvement in abuse and neglect, 133
 removal of Aboriginal children, 124, 133
Christian prayer, 104-5, 107, 110-11
Christians
 in Glasgow, 38
 media representation, 3
 scholarship, 33
citizenship ceremonies, 98
civil partnerships, 81-2, 84-5, 86, 88
conflict, and religion, 188-9
 *see also* violence; violent extremism
conscientious objection to work tasks, 78, 80-2, 84-5

council meetings, prayer and religious symbols, 103-5, 107, 110-11
Court of Justice of the EU (CJEU), 89-90
creation theology, 121, 123, 173-4
crosses/crucifixes
  *Eweida et al v the United Kingdom*, 80, 84, 87
  *Lautsi and others v Italy*, 105-6
  *Saguenay* case, 103-5, 107-8, 108-9, 112
culture, religion as, 103-8

## D

Dar al-Islam community centre, 66-7
definitions, of religion, 98-103
dementia care, 152
democracy, 5, 160
diasporic communities
  British Asian, 62-3
  Catholic-Cubans in Miami, 60, 61
  communal identity, 56
  complex diasporas, 57-8
  lived religion, 62
  locative and trans-locative orientations, 60-3, 64, 65, 66
  multilayered dichotomies, 55
  multilocality, 59-60, 62-3
  networks and power relations, 61, 64
  transnationalism, 67-8
  Twelver Shii Islam in Brent, 63-70
Dickson, Justice, 98-9
discrimination
  Asher's bakery, 83, 88
  bed and breakfast case, 82
  conscientious objection to work tasks, 78, 80-2, 84-5
  direct discrimination defined, 78
  direct vs indirect hierarchy, 88
  indirect discrimination defined, 10, 77-8
  refusal of services, 82-3
  religious dress at work, 79-80, 84, 87
domestic violence, 137-8
dress codes
  at work, 79-80, 84, 87
  Canadian citizenship ceremonies, 98
  in Swedish schools, 152
driver's licence case, 100

## E

education *see* religious education; schools
environment, and faith groups, 190
ethicality, and the environment, 190
equality
  equality law and freedom of religion tensions, 9, 77-8, 85-6
  EU directives, 89
  Equality Act (2010), 78, 88
  ethical citizenship, 34-5
  ethicality, new forms, 43
  European Commission, religion and welfare studies, 153-5
  European Convention on Human Rights (ECHR), 78, 79, 89
  European Court of Human Rights (ECtHR)
    discretion allowed to domestic courts, 89
    *Eweida et al v the United Kingdom*, 80, 84, 87
    *Lautsi and others v Italy*, 105-6
    religion as culture and heritage, 105-6
    work as public or private space, 87
  European Union
    Brexit, 6, 24, 65
    equality directives, 89
    lack of common standards on religion and belief, 89-90

evil, 41
*Eweida et al v the United Kingdom*, 80, 84, 87

## F

Fadlallah, Mohammad Hussein, 66
faith-based groups
  Australian welfare provision, 132-3, 137-9
  cooperation with secular organisations, 157-8
  and the environment, 190
  force for good, 160
  importance in postsecular world, 42, 43-4
  Nordic welfare provision, 150, 153-5, 160-1
  Oslo Forum for Dialogue and Cooperation, 157, 161-2
  outreach activities, 64
  public funding, 158-60
  social progress, 191
  social welfare provision, 9, 20, 42, 132-3, 134-5, 175-6, 189
  state recognition, 62
  for young people, 155-8
Faiths Forum for London, 65
family life, erosion, 23
feminist theory, 34, 37
financial crisis (2008), 6, 22, 24
France
  Charlie Hebdo attack, 18
  headscarves ban, 89
Francis, Pope, 190
freedom of religion, 9, 77-8, 83, 85-6, 189
fundamentalism, 5, 44, 115, 187
  *see also* violent extremism

## G

gay marriage
  Asher's bakery case, 83, 88
  civil partnerships case, 81-2, 84-5, 86, 88
  public opinion, 133
  *Reference re Same-Sex Marriage*, 111
geographies of religion, 33-6, 44-6, 177-8
Geography, 20-1
globalisation, 4, 5-6, 31

## H

Habermas, J.
  limitations of legal systems in settler colonial states, 115, 117, 119
  postsecular repentance, 116-17
  postsecularity, 5, 30, 42
  privacy of religion and the public sphere, 4-5, 179
Al-Hashimi, Ali, 64
hate crimes, 65
headscarves, 79, 80, 86, 152
hope, 41
human rights
  and equality laws, 9, 77-8, 85-6
  and religion, 189
  and religious traditions, 121, 124, 126
  UN Universal Declaration, 9, 125
Human Rights Act (1998), 79
Husayn ibn Ali, 68
Hussainiat al-Rasool al-Adham, 69
*Hutterian Brethren* (driver's licences), 100

## I

Indigenous peoples
  difficulties of integration, 115, 116, 117
  disadvantaged in settler colonial states, 115-16, 117, 119-20, 122
  historic injustices, 116
  Ktunaxa Nation, 101-2
  land rights, 101-2, 117-18, 125
  and public policy, 117, 124
  removal of children, 124, 133
  renewed attention, 95-6
  reparations for past injustices, 115, 117

restorative justice strategies, 117-18, 122-3, 123-4, 126
Rhode Island settlement, 125
rights, 173-4
scholarship on religion needed, 46
spirituality, 101-2, 121-2, 124, 173-4
UN Declaration on the Rights of Indigenous Peoples, 118, 119, 126

interdisciplinarity
Anthropology, 18-20
challenge posed by religion, 29-30, 180
Critical Geography, 20-1
Political Philosophy, 21-2
Religious Studies, 25-6
research methodology, 16-17
Social and Public Policy, 27
Theology, 22-4

interfaith initiatives, 65, 67, 157, 161-2, 179
International Panel on Social Progress (IPSP), 184-91
Iran, and Shiraziyyin rituals, 69-70
Iraq
Dawa Party, 66-7
Karbala, 68
Shii diaspora, 63, 66-7
*Ishaq v Canada (Citizenship and Immigration)*, 98
Islam
Al-Khoei Foundation, 64-5
Dar al-Islam community centre, 66-7
Hussainiat al-Rasool al-Adham, 69
mosque-synagogue joint festival, 65
resurgence, 5
Twelver Shii Islam, 63-70
Islamic Unity Forum, 67
Israel, Sykes-Picot Agreement, 67
Italy, *Lautsi and others v Italy*, 105-6

## J

Jehovah's Witnesses, 98
Jewish diaspora, 56
Jordanian Royal Institute for Inter-Faith Studies, 64
Judaism
Sukkot festival, 65, 102
synagogue-mosque joint festival, 65

## K

Karbala, 68
Khamenei, Sayyid Ali, 69
Khomeini, Ayatollah, 69
King, Martin Luther, 121-2
*Ktunaxa Nation v British Columbia*, 101-2

## L

*Ladele v Islington Borough Council*, 81-2, 84-5, 86, 88
land rights, 101-2, 117-18, 125
*Laudato Si'*, 190
*Lautsi and others v Italy*, 105-6
law
challenges and opportunities, 174
direct discrimination defined, 78
and equality, 9
indirect discrimination defined, 77-8
protection for religion and belief, 9, 77-8
religion as culture and heritage, 103-8
rights-based approach, 174
tensions between equality law and freedom of religion, 9, 77-8, 85-6
*see also* legal cases
*Lee v McArthur & Ors*, 83
left politics, decline, 20
legal cases
*Arrowsmith v UK*, 84
case law lists, 93-4, 114

## INDEX

conscientious objection to work tasks, 78, 80-2, 84-5
and core beliefs, 84-5
definitions of religion, 98-103
dress codes at work, 79-80, 84, 87
of everyday life, 96
indigenous religion, 101-2
*Mabo* (native title), 117-18
practical balance in UK, 80
proportionality approach, 81, 82, 88-9, 90-2, 173
refusal of services, 82-3
religion as culture and heritage, 103-8
Sunday as day of rest, 99
variable approach in Europe, 89-90
liminality, 30
lived religion, 34, 36-8, 46, 62, 103
*Loyola High School v Quebec*, 100-1, 112
Lutheran Church, 146-7, 149-50, 156

## M

*Mabo* case, 117-18
magic, 46
marriage *see* civil partnerships; gay marriage
media, 3, 133-4
Miami, Catholic-Cuban identity, 60, 61
Middle East, pan-Islamism, 67
migration
  Muslim migrants, 56, 153
  Nordic countries, 147
  and religious diversity, 4, 95, 187-8
  resurgence of global religion, 5
  *see also* diasporic communities
Minchin, Nick, 118-19
mindfulness, 28
modernity, 5-6, 20-1, 23-4
Mosques and Imams National Advisory Board (MINAB), 65

multiculturalism
  in Britain, 62
  in Canada, 105, 108-9
  and religion, 179
  and state neutrality, 112
Muslims
  British Islam and the *umma*, 58, 68
  media representation, 3
  migrants, 56, 153
  Muslim women, 38
  Swedish welfare support, 153

## N

nation-states, and the diaspora, 57, 58
neocolonialism, 67
neoliberalism, 5, 23, 44
new materialism, 22
New Zealand, earthquake, 41
Nicholls, Douglas, 121-2
non-religion
  growth in the West, 19-20
  and identity, 178
  increased interest, 28
  role in developing common good, 176
  semi-secularity, 148-9
  *see also* atheism
Nordic countries
  immigration, 147
  NOREL research on religion in the public sphere, 147-8
  religious complexity, 146-9
  state rather than faith group welfare, 149-51
  *see also* Norway; Sweden
Norway
  Church of Norway, 147, 156
  limited secular-religious cooperation, 157-8
  Oslo Forum for Dialogue and Cooperation, 157, 161-2
  religious membership trends, 147, 148, 156

Youth at the Margins survey, 156-8

## P

Paganism, 28
peace-making, 188-9
Pentecostal Christianity, 5, 40
performativity, 45
pilgrimage, 35, 45, 56, 177
policy *see* public policy
Political Geography, 34
Political Philosophy, 21-2
politics
  common life politics, 24
  decline of left politics, 20
populism, 6, 172
post-Christendom, 31
post-neoliberalism, 24
postcolonial theory, 34, 37
postcolonialism, settler colonial states, 115-16, 117, 119-20, 122-3
postsecularity
  contested concept, 30-1, 43, 172-3
  elements, 5
  and ethical spaces, 21, 122-3
  landscapes, 42-4
poststructural ethics, 37
prayer, 104-5, 107, 110-11
prohibitionism, 133--134
public policy
  opportunities and risks, 8-9, 171-3
  practice implications of religious diversity, 9-11
  and religious literacy, 27, 175
  and social progress, 190-1
public sphere
  care services, 152
  and diasporas, 58
  and privacy of religion, 4-5, 179
  and religion, 177-8
  and religious activities, 97-8
  religious complexity, 147-9

workplace and, 87
*see also* sacred spaces; workplace

## Q

Quebec
Jehovah's Witnesses, 98
*Saguenay* case, 103-5, 107-8, 108-9, 112

## R

*R v Big M Drug Mart Ltd*, 98-9
*R v Morgentaler*, 111
Ranson, D., 138-9
reconciliation, 102, 118, 122-3
*Reference re Same-Sex Marriage*, 111
religion
  and common good, 176
  communal aspects, 100-1
  definitions, 185-6
  and education, 97
  good/bad binary, 174-5
  legal definitions, 98-103
  lived religion, 34, 36-8, 46, 62, 103, 185-6
  majoritarian religions, 103-8, 111
  membership trends, 9, 95, 147, 148, 156
  multifaith initiatives, 65, 67, 157, 161-2, 179
  persistence, 190
  and social progress, 185-6
religious belief
  core belief, 84-5
  fluidity, 175, 178
  Nordic countries, 148-9
  simultaneity, 148-9
  sincerity of belief, 100, 102-3, 112
  spiritual capital, 176-7
  without belonging, 4
religious diversity, 4, 95, 187-8
religious education
  GCSE curriculum in Islam, 65
  in schools and universities, 28
  social workers, 135-6, 140

# INDEX

religious landscapes
  lived religious landscapes, 36-8
  sacred spaces, 35-6, 45-6, 56, 177-8
  spiritual, 38-41
religious literacy
  as democratic competence, 151
  for graduates, 26
  lacking, 3
  organisational perspective, 146, 161-2
  and public policy, 27, 175
  social work/workers, 139-40, 152, 176
religious organisations *see* faith-based groups
Religious Studies, 25-6, 59
  *see also* Theology and Religious Studies
religious symbols
  Canadian courts, 97, 103-5
  and human rights, 78, 79
  *Lautsi and others v Italy*, 105-6
  *see also* crosses/crucifixes; dress codes
religious visibility, 3, 7, 26-7, 148
religious-secular boundaries, 23-4, 29, 42, 174
research methodology, 15-17
restorative justice, 117-18, 122-3, 123-4, 126
Rhode Island, 125
rituals, Shiraziyyin, 68-70
*Rodriguez v British Columbia*, 111

# S

sacred spaces, 35-6, 45-6, 56, 177-8
al- Sadr, Muhammad Baqir, 66
*Saguenay* case, 103-5, 107-8, 108-9, 112
schools
  Canadian court cases, 97
  *Loyola High School v Quebec*, 100-1, 112
  and religious teaching, 27-8, 28
  school text books, 111-12
  *see also* religious education
secularism
  opportunities and challenges, 22-4, 28
  religious-secular boundaries, 23-4, 29, 42, 174
secularization thesis, 4, 20-1
self-flagellation, 69
sexual orientation
  bed and breakfast discrimination, 82, 88
  case law hierarchy, 88
  civil partnerships, 81-2, 84-5, 86, 88
  and marriage equality, 133
  refusal of services cases, 82-3, 88
  same-sex couples legal cases, 82-3, 111-12
al-Shirazi, Muhammad, 69-70
al-Shirazi, Sadiq, 70
Shiraziyyin, 68-70
Sikhs, turbans, 98
Social and Cultural Geography, 34
Social and Public Policy, 26-7
social progress
  and faith-based groups, 191
  International Panel, 184-91
  and religion, 185-6
social work/workers
  code of ethics, 136-7
  definition, 134
  partnerships with religious organisations, 137-9
  in the public sphere, 152
  religious beliefs, 135-6, 140-1
  and religious literacy, 139-40, 152, 176
  training, 135-6, 140
  *see also* welfare provision
Sociology, 4, 20
Sociology of Religion, 27-9
space
  and diaspora communities, 59-61, 70-1, 177
  public spaces, 177-8

public vs private in law, 87
spaces of religion, 34
spiritual capital, 176-7
spiritual landscapes, 34-5, 38-41, 45-6
Spiritualism, 39-40
spirituality, 101-2, 121-2, 124, 173-4, 179
state
  duty of religious neutrality, 105, 107, 109-10, 112
  religious-secular boundaries, 23-4, 29, 42, 174
  welfare provision, 149-51
Sufi shrines, 56
Sunday, as day of rest, 99
Supreme Court (Canada)
  abortion, 111
  *Amselem* case, 99-100, 102-3
  assisted death, 111
  *Big M Drug Mart* case, 98-9
  definitions of religion, 98-103
  *Hutterian Brethren* (driver's licence) case, 100
  interveners' religious voice, 111-12
  Ktunaxa beliefs, 101-2
  religious cases summaries, 97, 114
  *Saguenay* case, 105, 107-8, 108-9, 112
  school text books, 111-12
Supreme Court (UK), *Bull & Anor v Hall & Anor*, 82, 88
Sutherland, C., 37
Sweden
  democracy and election information, 160
  financial support for faith agencies, 158-60
  healthcare chaplaincy, 159
  Lutheran Church, 146-7, 149-50
  Muslim congregations, 153
  religious membership trends, 147, 148
  support in crisis situations, 159
  welfare provision, 154-5

Swedish Agency for Support to Faith Communities (SST), 158-61
Sykes-Picot Agreement, 67
*Syndicat Northcrest v Amselem*, 99-100, 102-3

## T

terrorism, Charlie Hebdo attack, 18
theography, 37
Theology, 22-4
Theology and Religious Studies, 7-8, 20, 22-4
Tomlins, S., 109
transnationalism, 67-8
Trump, Donald, 6, 24
Tutu, Desmond, 121-2

## U

United Nations
  Declaration on the Rights of Indigenous Peoples, 118, 119, 126
  Human Rights Council, 64
  Special Rapporteur on Freedom of Religion and Belief, 189
  Universal Declaration of Human Rights, 9, 125, 189
United States, Catholic-Cubans in Miami, 61
utilitarianism, 116, 125

## V

veiling (headscarves), 79, 80, 86, 152
violence
  domestic violence, 137-8
  gender-based, 179
  hate crimes, 65
violent extremism, 18, 26-7, 173, 187

## W

welfare provision

by faith groups, 9, 20, 42, 132-3, 134-5, 175-6, 189
majority religions, 153-4
marginal young people, 155-8
Nordic complexity, 146-9
religious minority organisations, 154-5
religious organisations in private sphere, 152-5
religious organisations seen as irrelevant, 175-6
state vs faith communities, 149-51
Western Europe research projects, 153-5
*see also* social work/workers
Wicca, 28
witchcraft, 46
women
  and domestic violence, 137-8
  Muslim women, 38
  and religion, 187
  religiosity, 37
workplace
  conscientious objection to work tasks, 78, 80-2, 84-5
  dress codes, 79-80, 84, 87
  public vs private space, 87

# Y

Yemen, civil war, 67
Youth at the Margins (YOMA) study, 155-8